Contents

THE November edition of JOHNSTONE is dedicated solely to the ongoing genocide in Gaza because, quite frankly, that's all we could think about this month. Each day has served up new and fresh horrors for our eyeballs as the worst massacre of this century dovetailed with social media and we all found ourselves with a front seat to rolling atrocities.

All works are written by Caitlin Johnstone and Tim Foley. The Caitlin Johnstone project is 100 percent reader-funded.

Visit **caitlinjohnst.one** for the original articles and their supporting links.

Tone Policing Opposition To Genocide

US senator Chris Coons sat across from journalist Aaron Maté on the train, which is about the worst place you could possibly choose to sit if you're a powerful official in a government that's in the middle of backing an active genocide.

As any journalist of sound conscience would, Maté seized the opportunity to begin questioning Coons on camera about his support for Israel's ongoing massacre of civilians in Gaza and to ask him why he isn't supporting a ceasefire.

Coons immediately became indignant that Maté was questioning him. He avoided addressing the questions he was being asked for a long time, responding only to repeatedly demand that Maté cease talking to him and to ask him who he is and how he got a seat on the train.

"This is a quiet car," Coons admonished.

"I understand, but children are dying sir," Maté replied. "They're being killed with our weapons. US weapons are killing kids in Gaza."

"Please stop," Coons kept repeating, ignoring the irony that "please stop" is all anyone is asking of the US-backed human butchery that is taking place in Gaza.

As British rapper and activist Lowkey noted on Twitter, Coons has received over a quarter million dollars from pro-Israel lobbying groups over the years.

Over and over and over again Coons tried to make the exchange about how Maté is being inappropriate and unprofessional and speaking the wrong way in the wrong venue, instead of the fact that the US government is directly funding and supplying a genocidal massacre that has killed thousands of children and displaced hundreds of thousands of people.

When all of this is over most of us will have regrets that we didn't do more, but Aaron Maté won't be among them.

I recommend watching the clip of the exchange if you haven't seen it yet, because it's such a perfect illustration of the way opposition to Israel's Gaza massacre is being aggressively tone policed by those who support it. Ever since the mass slaughter of Gazans began last month there's been a freakish trend

of working to shut down opposition to this atrocity by attacking the way people are opposing it, rather than attempting to address their concerns.

One good example of this was British prime minister Rishi Sunak's statement ahead of a peace march scheduled for Armistice Day, claiming to plan such a demonstration on that date was "provocative and disrespectful". Sure Rishi, Armistice Day is a completely inappropriate time for demonstrators to be literally calling for an armistice.

A recent tweet by Rupa Marya, an Associate Professor of Medicine with the University of California in San Francisco reads, "I'm going to remember forever the day that Israel was shelling hospitals, killing fleeing refugees and shutting off the electricity for NICU babies in incubators, the president of UC system sent us an email expressing concern about anti-Semitism & telling us to behave ourselves."

This is another good example of what I'm trying to point to here. People are trying to stop an active genocide and the leaders of western institutions keep trying to make the conversation about whether or not those efforts are "antisemitic", which none of them seem to be able to define in a way that is distinct from criticism of the Israeli government for war crimes and well-documented atrocities.

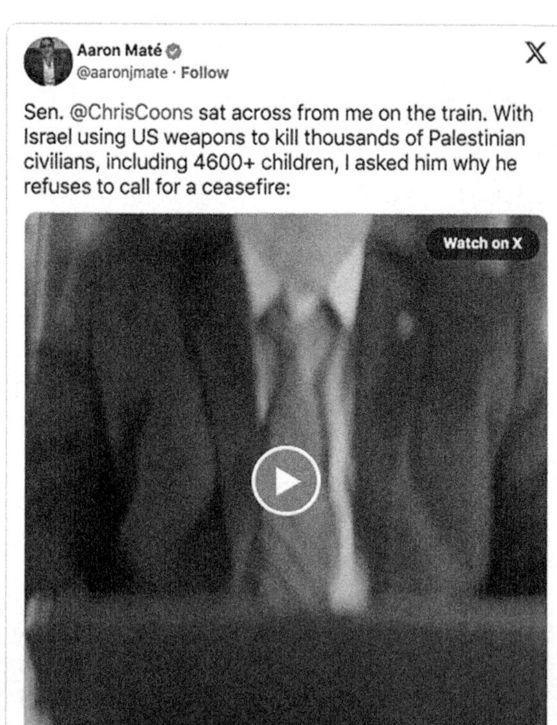

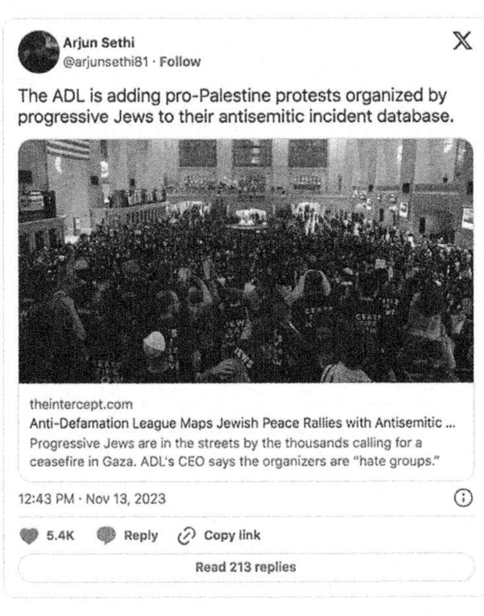

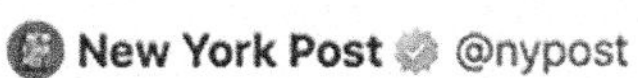

A few days ago The New York Times ran a front-page article titled "After Antisemitic Attacks, Colleges Debate What Kind of Speech Is Out of Bounds," which opens with a story about a Jewish college freshman having the horrible horrifying antisemitic experience of seeing a poster on campus which referred to Gaza as a "modern-day concentration camp". The Times quotes the student who underwent this unspeakable trauma as saying the mood on campus "is not pro-Palestinian, it's antisemitic."

For the record many experts agree that Gaza can rightly be described as a giant concentration camp, not least among them the great Jewish scholar Norman Finkelstein. But rather than discuss the abuses which gave rise to this crisis in the first place, outlets like The New York Times are working to make the conversation about antisemitism instead.

New reports from Mintpress News and The Intercept reveal that the massive 400 percent increase in antisemitic incidents across the United States that the mass media keep reporting is a statistic from the Anti Defamation League which includes pro-Palestine demonstrations as instances of antisemitism—even demonstrations by Jewish organizations. It turns out if you label all opposition to Israel "antisemitism" and then Israel murders thousands of children, you will inevitably see a large spike in "antisemitism" as you defined it.

Really this is all just garden variety manipulation by the western empire to shut down opposition to the political status quo. Any time a large movement emerges in opposition to the agendas of the ruling power structure you see the information ecosystem flooded with highly amplified concern trolls wagging their fingers at the tone and tactics of the movement to try and kill off the energy and drag the whole thing into inert pedantic quibbling.

That's what you're seeing with all the concern trolling about the popular chant "From the river to the sea, Palestine will be free," by the way. Palestinian rights activists will tell you the phrase means they want all Palestinians to be free from tyranny and abuse, and at most that they support the dismantling of the apartheid regime of Israel, but Israel supporters will look you dead in the eye and insist that the chant is a call for the genocide of Jewish people. In reality it's no more a call for genocide than supporting the end of Nazi Germany or apartheid South Africa was a call for genocide, but they re-interpret the slogan in the most negative way possible to mean something the people saying it have never intended, and then the powerful institutions of the western world start treating it like a hate crime.

All of this is just a large-scale version of the manipulation employed by Senator Coons on the train to get Aaron Maté to stop talking to him. It's all designed to divert attention away from the actual crime that is happening and get people shaking their fists at the specific methods of the people who oppose that crime. The whole objective is to grind the conversation down into insignificant quibbling about manners and decorum so people stop drawing attention to the blood-spattered elephant in the room.

And of course another reason the powerful place so much emphasis on politeness and etiquette whenever they are confronted is because they are all acutely aware that there are a whole lot more of us than there

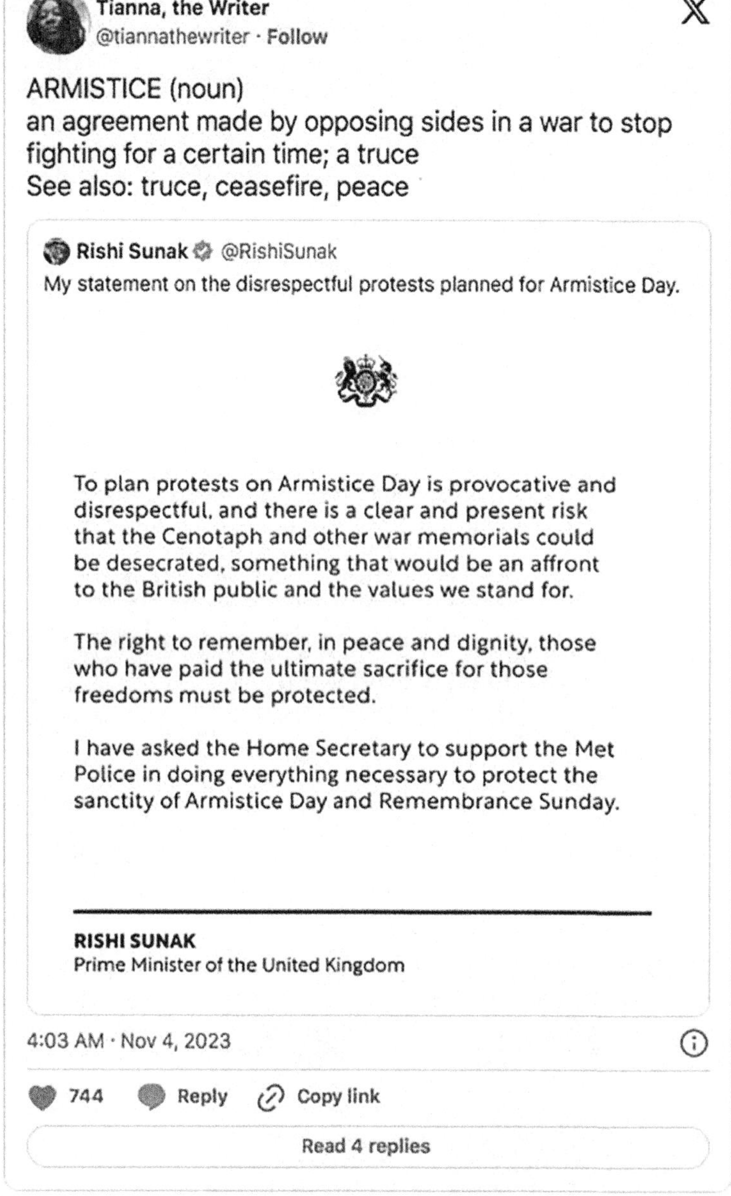

are of them, and that people can decide at any time to stop playing by the rules and simply tear down the ruling power structures which commit mass atrocities in their name. As long as everyone's worried about being perceived as sufficiently well-mannered, the people will never awaken to their true power.

.

Israelis Keep Hurting Their Own PR Interests By Talking

One problem Israel keeps running into is how the institutionalized dehumanization of Palestinians which keeps the apartheid state operational also causes Israelis to say things that non-Israelis will find extremely shocking, which hurts Israel's PR interests.

We saw this illustrated in a recent New Yorker interview with Daniella Weiss, a leader of the push to build illegal Israeli settlements on Palestinian land. Weiss stated frankly and unapologetically that she supports apartheid, that she doesn't believe Palestinians should have any sovereignty anywhere, that she doesn't believe Palestinians should have voting rights, that she wants the population of Gaza to be replaced by Israeli settlements, and that she is untroubled by the killing of children in Gaza because she feels it's being done in the interests of Israeli children.

Asked where the Palestinians in Gaza should go, Weiss replied, "To Sinai, to Egypt, to Turkey." When the interviewer said the Palestinians are not Egyptian or Turkish, she contended that "The Ukrainians are not French, but when the war started they went to many countries."

To the question "When you see Palestinian children dying, what's your emotional reaction as a human being?", Weiss answered, "I go by a very basic human law of nature. My children are prior to the children of the enemy, period. They are first. My children are first."

Asked if she believes human rights are not universal and should not apply equally to everyone, Weiss replied "That's right."

But perhaps the most revealing statement Weiss made was her entirely truthful explanation of what drives the Israeli push to colonize Palestinian land:

"In Israel, there's a lot of support for settlements, and this is why there have been right-wing governments for so many years. The world, especially the United States, thinks there is an option for a Palestinian state, and, if we continue to build communities, then we block the option for a Palestinian state. We want to close the option for a Palestinian state, and the world wants to leave the option open. It's a very simple thing to understand."

That one paragraph right there will teach you more about the present-day realities of the Israel-Palestine conflict than an entire year of watching CNN. It's horrid, and it's jarring to hear it spoken out loud in a favorable way… but it's true.

This sort of thing has been happening for years. Israelis who've been marinating in a self-validating echo chamber of Zionist ideology which dehumanizes Palestinians and normalizes oppression and abuse don't think twice about saying things that make Israel look bad on the world stage, because to them it's just the standard status quo way of looking at things.

In 2021 a settler from New York named Yaakov Fauci made headlines around the world with his candid statements to a Palestinian family whose Sheikh Jarrah home he was squatting in.

Fauci, apparently fully aware that he was being filmed, famously replied to the family's complaints that he was stealing their home by shamelessly telling them, "If I don't steal it, someone else will steal it."

And the thing is, he wasn't lying. He was truthfully describing an abusive dynamic in apartheid Israel where Palestinians are being forced out of their homes in order to control ethnic demographics and advance the agenda outlined above by Daniella Weiss. If he'd been a trained propagandist for the Israeli state he never would have made such comments on camera, but because he was just a Zionism-indocrinated member of the Israeli public he saw no reason to hold his tongue.

Some years ago The Empire Files' Abby Martin put together

a devastating critique of the Zionist ideology just by going around the streets of Jerusalem with a camera and a microphone and talking to Jewish Israelis about their views on Palestinians. Over and over and over again they shared their support for tyranny, murder, genocide and ethnic cleansing in their own words and without hesitation, never thinking that their words could be used to harm Israel's image, because to them these were just normal things that they said all the time in their day to day life.

You see the same sort of thing when Israelis are filmed sitting in lawn chairs to watch and cheer IDF bombing operations on Palestinian neighborhoods, during which a woman once told the press "I'm just a little bit fascist" after advocating the total destruction of Gaza City.

Every time this happens it sends viral video footage around the internet and does real damage to the world's perception of Israel. That's a big part of why Israel is struggling to control the narrative about the Gaza massacre today, which is in turn being exacerbated by more incendiary statements by Israelis, not just from the general public but from within the Israeli government itself.

On Saturday Israeli security cabinet member and Agriculture Minister Avi Dichter casually referred to the violent forced expulsion of Palestinians from the northern half of the Gaza Strip as "Nakba 2023", a reference to the violent forced expulsion which was inflicted on Palestinians at the establishment of the Israeli state in 1948.

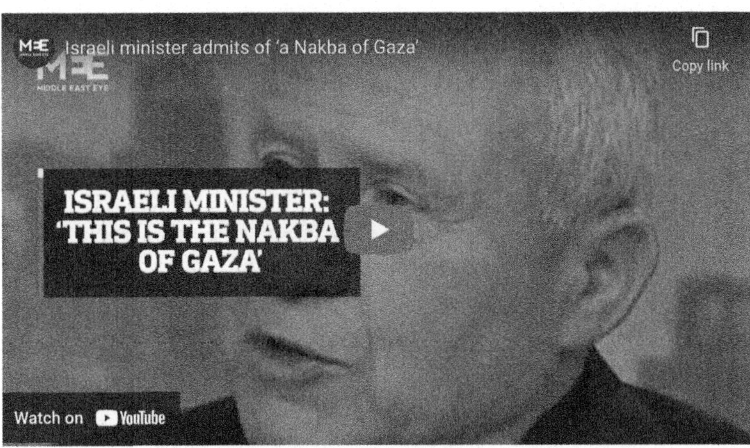

Haaretz reports:

Israeli security cabinet member and Agriculture Minister Avi Dichter (Likud) was asked in a news interview on Saturday whether the images of northern Gaza Strip residents evacuating south on the IDF's orders are comparable to images of the Nakba. He replied: "We are now rolling out the Gaza Nakba. From an operational point of view, there is no way to wage a war—as the IDF seeks to do in Gaza—with masses between the tanks and the soldiers."

When asked again whether this was the "Gaza Nakba", Dichter—a member of the security cabinet and former Shin Bet director—said "Gaza Nakba 2023. That's how it'll end."

When later asked if this means Gaza City residents won't be allowed to return, he replied: "I don't know how it'll end up happening since Gaza City is one-third of the Strip—half the land's population but a third of the territory."

Dichter's comments are surprising not only because Israel has been publicly framing the mass displacement in Gaza as

a measure taken solely to protect civilians, but also because the Israeli government has long officially denied that the Nakba ever happened, even passing laws forbidding its history to be taught in schools.

Even as western officials hasten to frame Israel's actions as a defensive and measured response to the Hamas attack on October 7, Israeli officials have been falling all over themselves in a mad rush to make those western officials look like liars.

When talking about the Gaza assault Prime Minister Benjamin Netanyahu made headlines by invoking the biblical nation of Amalek, whose people God instructed the Israelites to commit total genocide against. The first book of Samuel contains the instructions, "Now go, attack the Amalekites and totally destroy all that belongs to them. Do not spare them; put to death men and women, children and infants, cattle and sheep, camels and donkeys."

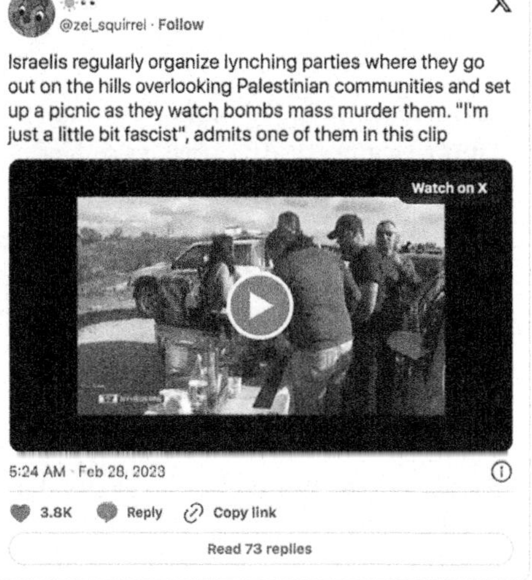

President Isaac Herzog insinuated last month that all civilians in Gaza are legitimate military targets because they failed to overthrow Hamas, saying, "It is not true this rhetoric about civilians not being aware, not involved. It's absolutely not true. They could have risen up. They could have fought against that evil regime which took over Gaza in a coup d'etat."

When announcing the total siege on Gaza which would see the enclave cut off from electricity, food, water and fuel, Israeli defense minister Yoav Gallant stated that "we are fighting human animals, and we are acting accordingly."

IDF spokesman Daniel Hagari said Israel would turn Gaza into a "city of tents" and that Israel's "emphasis is on damage and not on accuracy" in its bombing campaign.

Dan Gillerman, Israel's former ambassador to the UN, said last month that "I am very puzzled by the constant concern which the world is showing for the Palestinian people and is actually showing for these horrible, inhuman animals who have done the worst atrocities that this century has seen."

"Hamas became ISIS and the citizens of Gaza are celebrating instead of being horrified," The Economist cites an Israeli general saying last month. "Human beasts are dealt with accordingly."

"Creating a severe humanitarian crisis in Gaza is a necessary means to achieve the goal," a major general named Giora Eiland wrote in an Israeli newspaper, adding, "Gaza will become a place where no human being can exist."

Israel's allies keep trying to portray it as a rational actor and a positive force in the world, but if you listen to Israelis themselves you get a very different understanding of what this murderous apartheid state is actually about.

As Maya Angelou said, when someone shows you who they are, believe them the first time.

Image via Wikimedia Commons

US Says It's Powerless To Stop The Genocide That It Is Directly Funding And Supplying

In a bizarre new article titled "White House frustrated by Israel's onslaught but sees few options," The Washington Post reports that the Biden administration believes Israel has gone too far and is killing too many civilians in its assault on Gaza, but are powerless to do anything about it.

The Post's Yasmeen Abutaleb writes the following, citing anonymous US officials:

"As Israel's ground invasion of Gaza escalates, the Biden administration finds itself in a precarious position: Administration officials say Israel's counterattack against Hamas has been too severe, too costly in civilian casualties, and lacking a coherent endgame, but they are unable to exert significant influence on America's closest ally in the Middle East to change its course.

"U.S. efforts to get Israel to scale back its counterattack in response to the Oct. 7 killings by Hamas that left at least 1,400 Israelis dead have failed or fallen short. The Biden administration urged Israel against a ground invasion, privately asked it to consider proportionality in its attacks, advocated a higher priority on avoiding civilian deaths, and called for a humanitarian pause—only for Israeli officials to dismiss or reject all those suggestions.

...

"In recent days, they said, the administration has become deeply uncomfortable with some of Israel's tactics. Last week, Israel bombed the densely packed Jabalya refugee camp two days in a row, an attack that Israel said killed a Hamas leader but that also killed dozens of civilians. On Friday, an Israeli airstrike hit near the entrance of Al Shifa Hospital in Gaza City, a strike the Israeli military said was aimed at an ambulance 'being used by a Hamas terrorist cell.' And Israeli authorities recently expelled thousands of Palestinians who had been in Israel for work, sending them back into Gaza even as it continues to bomb the enclave."

All this helpless hand-wringing is exposed for the load of ridiculous bullshit that it plainly is a few paragraphs down in the very same article:

"Washington is Israel's largest military backer, and the White House has asked Congress for an additional $14 billion in aid for Israel in the wake of the Hamas attacks. But administration officials and advisers say the levers the United States theoretically has over Israel, such as conditioning military aid on making the military campaign more targeted, are nonstarters, partly because they would be so politically unpopular in any administration and partly because, aides say, Biden himself has a personal attachment to Israel."

So the Biden administration does in fact have tons of leverage it can use to stop the genocidal massacre in Gaza, it just doesn't want to because it would be "politically unpopular" and because "Biden himself has a personal attachment to Israel."

The US president does indeed have a personal attachment to Israel. Biden has proudly described himself as a Zionist, and has gone on record to say that if Israel didn't exist the United States would have to invent an Israel to advance its interests in the middle east.

In summary, this Washington Post article is telling us that Biden is powerless to stop the genocidal

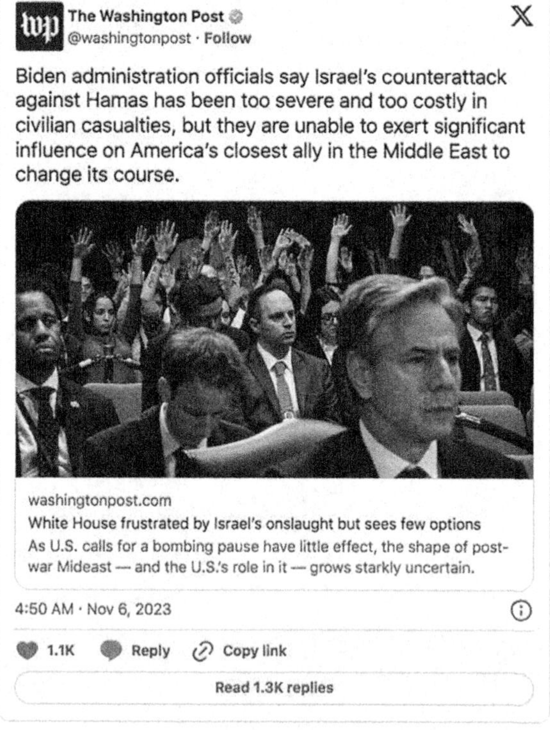

massacre in Gaza because he really likes the people doing the genocide and doesn't want to stop them from doing it.

We've been asked to believe a lot of very stupid things since this onslaught began last month, but the idea that the Biden administration is powerless to stop a genocide that it is directly arming and supplying has got to be the absolute stupidest.

Of course the US can stop this. Of course it can. The US is currently pouring weapons into Israel on an almost daily basis, is pouring billions of dollars into Israel and is preparing to pour in billions more, and is currently physically assisting Israeli operations in Gaza with drones and special operations forces while US warships swarm the eastern Mediterranean. All of this can easily be pulled away if Israel refuses to stop murdering children by the thousands in an indiscriminate bombing campaign that reportedly isn't even doing any meaningful damage to Hamas.

What's that? You didn't know this murderous bombing campaign is doing no meaningful damage to Hamas? Well let's clear that up then.

A new report by The New York Times cites an anonymous US military official saying that Israel "has not come close" to destroying Hamas leadership or even its mid-level command.

"One senior U.S. defense official, who spoke on condition of anonymity to discuss sensitive details, said the operations so far have not come close to destroying Hamas's senior and middle leadership ranks," The New York Times reports.

This revelation is devastating to the Israeli narrative about what it has actually been doing in Gaza. Israel said on Thursday that it had bombed some 12,000 targets in Gaza since October 7, and that number would be even higher by now, especially with unprecedented levels of strikes now being reported by people on the ground. There are reportedly only some 20-25,000 members of Hamas in total, which means the number of airstrikes is fast approaching the total number of Hamas members in existence, yet going from this New York Times report no meaningful damage has been done to Hamas itself.

This despite the fact that we are being told Hamas makes prevalent use of "human shields", hiding their units in clusters of civilians for protection. How has Israel managed to kill some ten thousand Palestinians in Gaza without managing to do any real damage to Hamas if Hamas fighters are hiding amongst all those civilians? You'd think by sheer law of averages they'd have taken out some significant leaders with all that civilian-massacring?

Maybe Hamas is using really high-level human shields, the kind that

Chris Megerian
@ChrisMegerian · Follow

"One senior U.S. defense official, who spoke on condition of anonymity to discuss sensitive details, said the operations so far have not come close to destroying Hamas's senior and middle leadership ranks."

nytimes.com
U.S. Officials Outline Steps to Israel to Reduce Civilian Casualties
The measures include using smaller bombs against Hamas, U.S. officials said.

11:46 PM · Nov 5, 2023

87   Reply   Copy link

Read 9 replies

don't even have any Hamas fighters hidden behind them. It's all 100 percent human shield with zero percent combatant—the most secure type of human shield there is!

The Washington Post report about Biden's imaginary powerlessness to stop this massacre makes a bit more sense when you look at an NBC News article which came out a few days earlier, which reports that White House leadership are concerned about an emerging "narrative" that Biden supports the killing in Gaza.

NBC News reports the following:

"Biden and his top aides have in the past week adjusted the administration's public message to emphasize concern for Palestinian civilians and U.S. efforts to get them humanitarian relief. The shift follows growing criticism at home and abroad of Biden's decision to swiftly and staunchly back Israel's military response to Hamas while initially speaking less forcefully about protecting Palestinians; meanwhile, images of civilian casualties in Gaza continue to ricochet around the world.

"'If this really goes bad, we want to be able to point to our past statements,' a senior U.S. official said. The official said the administration is particularly worried about a narrative taking hold that Biden supports all Israeli military actions and that U.S.-provided weapons have been used

to kill Palestinian civilians, many of them women and children. The Defense Department has said the U.S. is not putting any limits or restrictions on the weapons it's providing Israel."

So it's probably a safe bet that the anonymous US officials who spoke to The Washington Post about how "frustrated" the White House is with Israel's unbridaled murderousness are White House officials who are trying to manage the public narrative about Biden. They're trying to let the Biden White House wash its hands of this genocidal massacre like Pontius Pilate, even as it backs that very massacre to the hilt.

I have said it before and I'll say it again: the US is every bit as culpable for the murder of all these civilians as Israel. Don't let the empire's narrative managers try to tell you different.

Featured image via Adobe Stock.

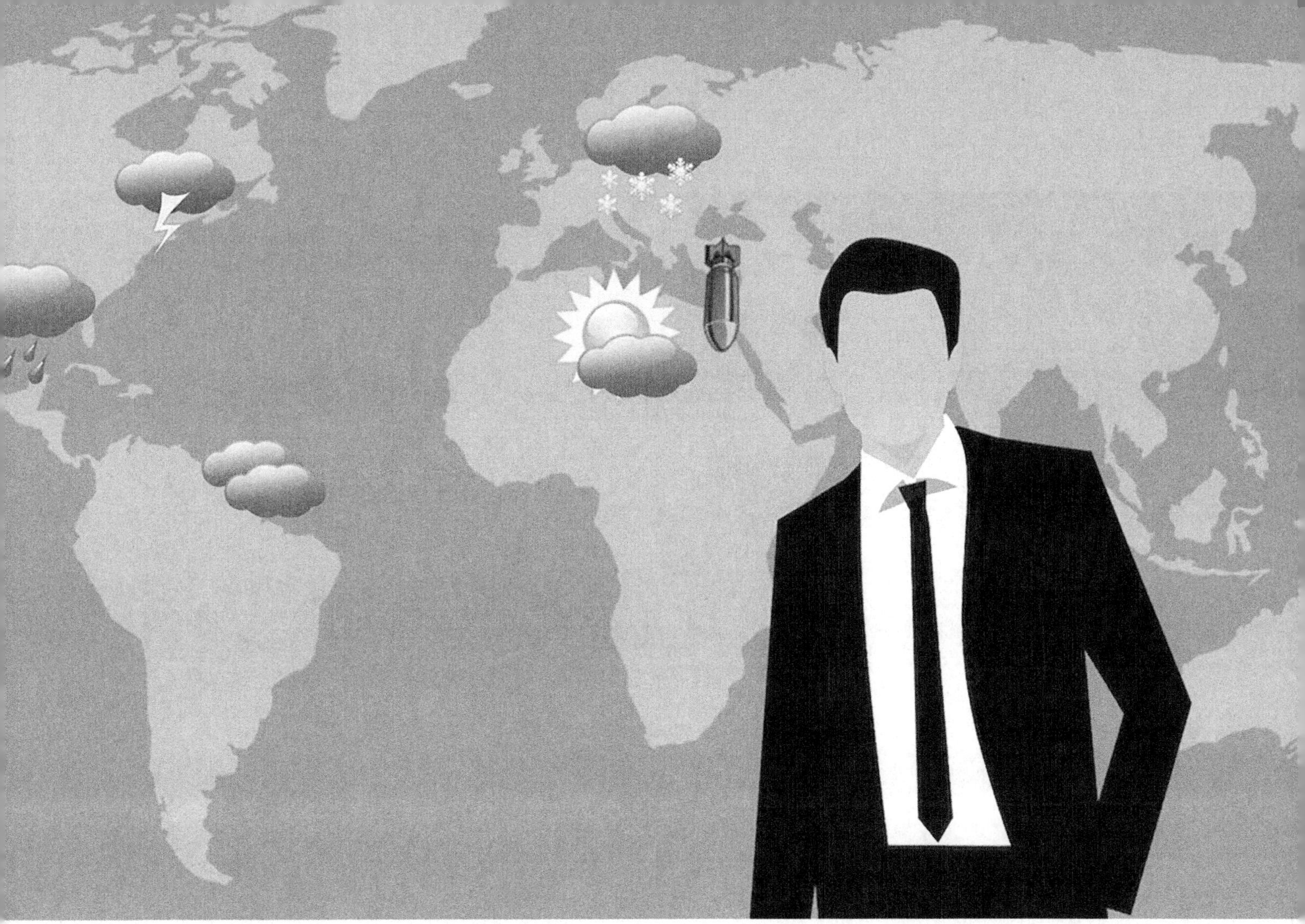

It's A Little Bit Bomby In Gaza Today

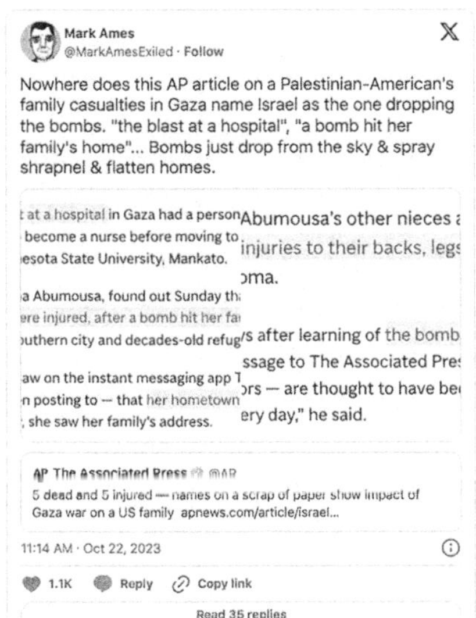

Mark Ames
@MarkAmesExiled · Follow

Nowhere does this AP article on a Palestinian-American's family casualties in Gaza name Israel as the one dropping the bombs. "the blast at a hospital", "a bomb hit her family's home"... Bombs just drop from the sky & spray shrapnel & flatten homes.

t at a hospital in Gaza had a person
become a nurse before moving to
esota State University, Mankato.

a Abumousa, found out Sunday th
ere injured, after a bomb hit her fa
outhern city and decades-old refug

aw on the instant messaging app T
n posting to — that her hometown
, she saw her family's address.

Abumousa's other nieces a
injuries to their backs, legs
oma.

s after learning of the bomb
ssage to The Associated Pres
ors — are thought to have be
ery day," he said.

AP The Associated Press @AP
5 dead and 5 injured — names on a scrap of paper show impact of Gaza war on a US family apnews.com/article/israel...

11:14 AM · Oct 22, 2023

1.1K Reply Copy link

Read 35 replies

It's a little bit bomby in Gaza today,
at least that's what the news men say.

Israeli victims were "murdered" and "killed"
and all mourn the innocent blood that was spilled,

but in Gaza explosives just fall from the air
and nobody mentions who launched them, from where.

They talk about "blasts" and how buildings were "hit".
Who blasted and hit them? Eh, who gives a shit.

It's a little bit bomby outside, that's the weather.
Put up your umbrellas, dudes. Get it together.

The US Empire's PR Crisis In Gaza
Notes From The Edge Of The Narrative Matrix

The US-centralized empire is a giant network of allies, partners and assets spanning the entire globe. Many of the nations in this network, such as Israel, have strong ideologies and values systems that the empire must cooperate with to obtain their loyalty. But the empire itself has no ideology or values—it values nothing but planetary domination. The empire's motives are no more ideological than the motives of a mugger are ideological.

So the empire has no ideology, but it is held together by cooperation with individual governments who do. The problem this creates is that sometimes the ideologies of those states cause them to do things that go against the interests of the empire as a whole. Israel can just up and decide to commit a genocidal massacre in front of everyone. Saudi Arabia can decide it's going to dismember a Washington Post reporter with a bone saw. Proxies in Ukraine can keep saying Nazi things and sporting Nazi insignia in public. They do these things because unlike the top brass in the imperial power structure they are guided by ideology, with no regard for the need to preserve the empire's image as a "rules-based international order".

This often creates a PR crisis for the empire, because the public will cease consenting to the network of alliances, partners and assets if it becomes sufficiently aware of the depravity needed to hold it all together. This is typically easy to resolve because the US empire has the most sophisticated propaganda machine in the history of civilization, but that propaganda machine is operated by individuals—individuals who may have learned about Palestinian rights at university, or who were disgusted about the way their employer ran cover for Israel's murder of Shireen Abu Akleh only to find out Israel did it and was lying. So they don't always play along with the imperial machine in their reporting, thereby exacerbating the empire's PR crisis.

The worst thing that could possibly happen, from the empire's point of view, is for the public to start opening their eyes to its criminality. With Israel on a genocidal rampage as pro-Palestinian protesters flood the streets worldwide, we may be certain that the manipulators who are responsible for imperial perception management are in full crisis mode, because if a critical mass of people can pick apart this one lie, it opens up the possibility of their unplugging themselves from the whole propaganda matrix that keeps the empire operational.

The empire managers are standing by Israel's side and doing everything they can to pretend its actions are right and just, but they are fidgeting uncomfortably, and behind the scenes we may be sure they're in total damage control. That's why we're being slammed with such a mad deluge of propaganda right now, and that's why they're doing everything they can to censor and suppress and shut down voices who are critical of Israel's actions in Gaza.

·

Hundreds of US congressional staffers are passing around a letter urging their bosses to call for a ceasefire, there's a silent mutiny brewing in the State Department over the Biden administration's Gaza actions, mainstream reporters have been refusing to parrot Israel narratives, and the streets are full of pro-Palestine demonstrators.

This is different. What we are seeing right now is a deviation from the usual script.

·

The western press have been finding themselves in the uncomfortable position of having to do reporting alongside the middle easterners they've been lying about for generations, and discovering that a lot of those middle easterners speak English and have a few things to say.

There's a clip going around of Egyptian podcaster Rahma Zein laying into CNN's Clarissa Ward at a protest at the Rafah Crossing border gates:

There's another viral clip of a Palestinian man telling off CNN's Sara Sidner—who helped circulate the infamous "40 decapitated babies" psyop—saying "You are genocide supporters! You are not welcome here! Genocide supporters! Fuck CNN! Fuck CNN!":

An urgently needed message and a long overdue confrontation.

.

If Israel didn't bomb that hospital then why did it doctor up a fraudulent audio clip pretending to show Hamas fighters saying Israel didn't bomb the hospital?

The only way to reconcile this fact with a belief in Israel's innocence is rigorous psychological compartmentalization.

.

A lot of the distortion around this current crisis arises from confusion between peace and the baseline status quo. Because Israel had been trucking along at the same status quo for so long, people assume there was a state of peace when Hamas attacked it, which was why the western political/media class were able to frame it as an "unprovoked" attack. But in reality the status quo in Israel has been one of continually escalating violence, tyranny and abuse for generations, not one of peace.

The trouble with abusive dynamics that have been going on for a long time is that after a while those who aren't directly affected by the abuse tend to get used to that way of being and start thinking of it as normal. So when there's pushback against that abusive status quo, it looks to them like it came completely out of nowhere at the hands of an unprovoked aggressor.

Stand on someone's face for long enough and one day it will surprise you if he eventually bites your foot. You might even feel like you were the victim, because that's just what you'd gotten used to.

And the imperial media of course do everything they can to exacerbate public confusion about this crucial distinction. The Hamas attack is being constantly framed as an unprovoked act of aggression by evil

Caitlin Johnstone ✓
@caitoz · Follow

Oh yeah well my six month-old baby just said "Israel is an abusive apartheid state that cannot exist without nonstop war and violence which is exactly why the US empire uses it as a military and intelligence proxy in a geostrategically crucial region it must dominate by force."

> Bethany S. Mandel ✓ @bethanyshondark
> "I don't want to be Jewish. They don't shoot non-Jews." - my four year old

8:45 AM · Oct 22, 2023

♥ 4K   Reply   Copy link

Read 74 replies

men who wanted to do evil things to Jews, solely because they are evil and hate Jews. History began on October 7, and all the events from 1948 onward never happened.

Empire propagandists do this constantly by the way, wherever it suits the information interests of the empire. After 9/11 it was "they hate us for our freedom" and all the US aggressions in the middle east which provoked Al Qaeda were swept under the carpet. When Russia invaded Ukraine the well-documented NATO provocations and violence in the Donbass which gave rise to it were written out of the history books, and history began on February 24, 2022. If China ever reacts to the US military surrounding it with war machinery and its aggressive provocations in Taiwan, that will be framed as a completely unprovoked attack which came completely out of nowhere as well.

Circumstances aren't peaceful just because we are used to them. Just because you are able to go about your daily routine without major disruption doesn't mean someone isn't being horrifically abused by the status quo which makes your way of life possible. Peace doesn't look like everyone complying with the status quo regardless of its abusiveness, it looks like the absence of abuse.

•

"Hey what do you do for a living Caitlin?"

"Oh these days I mostly accidentally look at footage of dead Palestinian kids on my social media feed and cry and get called an anti-semite."

•

If you didn't already know that Israel apologists use false accusations of anti-semitism to shut down criticism of Israel, you should know it now. When they're trying to tell you Greta Thunberg is a closet Nazi sending out obscure Nazi dogwhistles, it's right there in your face.

•

If someone asked me to design the absolute worst place anyone could possibly detonate thousands of explosive munitions on, I'd probably come up with a densely populated area full of easily collapsed buildings wherein an extremely high percentage of the population are children.

•

It should be clear to everyone by now that a huge percentage of the right wingers who criticized US proxy warfare via Ukraine did so only because they were worried it might take away from US proxy warfare via Israel.

•

One of the reasons this specific bombing campaign is getting so much more public backlash than others is because the pro-Palestine movement has had generations to build, whereas when the US empire lays waste to a country using military explosives it's normally a fast ordeal which moves from manufacturing consent to execution very quickly. By the time people figure out they were lied to about the justifications for a depraved war the empire is usually two or three new wars down the track. The

Israel-Palestine issue has been just sitting there for decades, so there's been time to accumulate popular opposition. Once someone learns about the realities of the Palestinian plight they very seldom abandon their support for it, so every newly-opened pair of eyes stays open on this issue for a lifetime.

Another major reason is because of humanity's exponentially expanded ability to rapidly share information in recent years. Palestinians have become able to record the abuses of Israeli apartheid and bombing campaigns on their phones and upload them onto the internet, where they rapidly circulate on social media. This ability to rapidly circulate raw video footage has played a major role in Israel's PR problem in recent years, because there's nothing an Israel apologist can say that will have more impact than raw footage of an Israeli settler telling a Palestinian family that he stole their home because "If I don't steal it, someone else is gonna steal it." This killed off a lot of public sympathy for Israel in the lead-up to the current onslaught.

Another reason is because the pro-Palestine movement was carried on the tide of the global movement against apartheid South Africa, giving the world a framework to understand Israeli abuses and helping to build the base of a related cause.

Another reason is because many of us in colonized countries like Australia, the US and Canada recognize the patterns of what's happening in Israel and see that there's an opportunity for human history to get it right this time before the genocide machine really gets going.

Another reason is because it's been widely accepted by western society that racism is a bad thing and the abuses which led to this particular bombing campaign are so clearly fueled by racism.

Another reason is because the abuses of the Israeli regime are so glaringly obvious and uncomplicated that they can override all the propaganda and cognitive biases we are swimming in in western civilization. All most people need is to really see it and wrap their minds around what they're seeing, and truth does the rest of the work for them. That was the case before the Gaza massacre began, and it's so much more so now.

Image by Adobe Stock

Israel Apologists Relentlessly Gaslight And Attack Our Sense Of Reality

The Atlantic has a new Israel apologia article out titled "The Decolonization Narrative Is Dangerous and False"—a noticeable change in tone from the outlet's "Decolonize Russia" sentiments of last year.

The entire article has been picked apart paragraph by paragraph by a commentator named Sana Saeed, but for my purposes here I'd just like to focus on one specific sentence in it about Israel's ongoing massacre in Gaza:

"The Israeli goal in Gaza—for practical reasons, among others—is to minimize the number of Palestinian civilians killed."

If you didn't know that The Atlantic's editor-in-chief Jeffrey Goldberg is a former IDF prison guard who in 2002 said that "the coming invasion of Iraq will be remembered as an act of profound morality", it would astonish you that such a sentence ever went to print.

One need only look at the before and after satellite images of the bombing campaign in Gaza to see immediately that Israel is doing nothing at all to minimize the number of civilians killed.

One need only look at the fact that nearly 70 percent of the people killed in these airstrikes have been women and children to see immediately that Israel is doing nothing to minimize the number of civilians killed.

One need only listen to Israeli officials themselves saying "the emphasis is on damage and not on accuracy" and "Gaza will eventually turn into a city of tents; there will be no buildings" to see immediately that Israel is doing nothing to minimize the number of civilians killed.

You don't get to openly declare that you're going to do a ton of damage with no regard for accuracy, carpet bomb entire neighborhoods into gravel killing mostly women and children, and then say you're trying to minimize civilian casualties. That's not a thing.

But that's exactly what The Atlantic instructs us to believe. They demand that we ignore what's right in front of our faces and mistrust what we are seeing with our own eyes.

You see this kind of thing over and over again from Israel apologists. They tell you things you absolutely know to be false in your own direct perception, over and over and over again, in the hope that they can overwhelm your mind. That's what's happening when they tell you Israel is "defending itself" and "targeting Hamas" when they're mostly killing women and children and bombing entire city blocks into powder, and that's what's happening when they tell you over and over again that you hate Jews and love terrorists even when you know for a fact that you don't.

The term "gaslighting" has been frequently misused in modern political discourse lately; you'll often see people using that term to describe someone lying, or even someone just saying something they don't agree with. But that's not what the term gaslighting historically means.

Merriam-Webster defines gaslighting as "psychological manipulation of a person usually over an extended period of time that causes the victim to question the validity of their own thoughts, perception of reality, or memories". It's when you attack someone's perception of reality with such sustained aggression that the victim's psyche just kind of gives up and assumes they're not mentally competent enough to interpret reality for themselves.

And that's exactly what you see Israel apologists doing day in and day out with regard to this conflict.

They tell you to doubt your own eyes when you see mountains upon mountains of evidence that Israel is raining high tech military explosives upon areas known to be packed full of children.

They tell you to doubt your own ears when Israeli officials spout genocidal rhetoric.

They tell you to doubt your own intelligence when you talk about the many gaping plot holes in what we're told to believe about October 7.

They tell you to doubt your own sanity when they demand that you

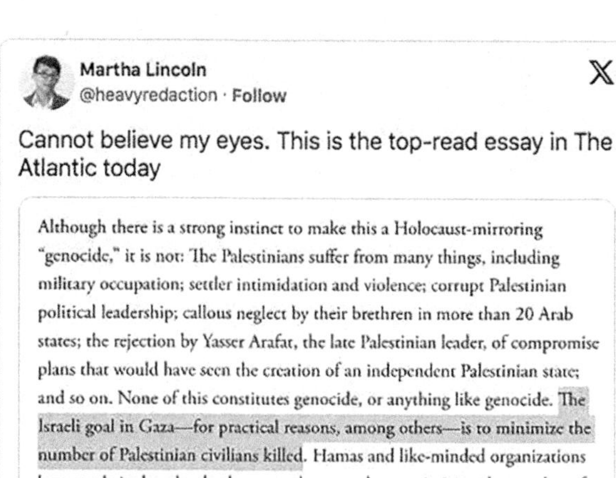

Martha Lincoln
@heavyredaction · Follow

Cannot believe my eyes. This is the top-read essay in The Atlantic today

Although there is a strong instinct to make this a Holocaust-mirroring "genocide," it is not: The Palestinians suffer from many things, including military occupation; settler intimidation and violence; corrupt Palestinian political leadership; callous neglect by their brethren in more than 20 Arab states; the rejection by Yasser Arafat, the late Palestinian leader, of compromise plans that would have seen the creation of an independent Palestinian state; and so on. None of this constitutes genocide, or anything like genocide. The Israeli goal in Gaza—for practical reasons, among others—is to minimize the number of Palestinian civilians killed. Hamas and like-minded organizations have made it abundantly clear over the years that maximizing the number of Palestinian casualties is in their strategic interest. (Put aside all of this and consider: The world Jewish population is still smaller than it was in 1939, because of the damage done by the Nazis. The Palestinian population has grown, and continues to grow. Demographic shrinkage is one obvious marker of genocide. In total, roughly 120,000 Arabs and Jews have been killed in the conflict over Palestine and Israel since 1860. By contrast, at least 500,000 people, mainly civilians, have been killed in the Syrian civil war since it began in 2011.)

2:06 PM · Oct 28, 2023

3K   Reply   Copy link

Read 125 replies

accept unverified allegations about beheaded babies and babies cooked in ovens while ignoring the thousands of children that are being massacred in Gaza.

They tell you to doubt your own beliefs when they tell you repeatedly that you're an anti-semite for criticizing Israel even when you know you have nothing but good will toward Jewish people.

They tell you to doubt your own motives when they tell you repeatedly that you support terrorism and want Jews to be killed even when you know nothing could be further from the truth.

They tell you to doubt your sense of reality when they tell you Hamas is responsible for all the death and destruction that you can plainly see is being inflicted by Israeli bombs.

They're never just telling you what to believe about the world, they're also telling you what to believe about yourself. This is always a telltale sign that you are being psychologically manipulated. Anytime you find yourself involved with someone who continually works to change your perception of yourself in a negative way, you would be well-advised to dis-involve yourself from them as quickly as possible.

Israel apologists need to do this because they don't have truth on their side, and they don't have morality on their side, so all they've got is manipulation. They work so hard to distort your perception of reality because a lucid perception of reality is highly unfavorable to Israeli information interests.

Don't let them do this to you. Whenever you get the sense that you are being manipulated by someone, just start ignoring their words and watch their actions instead. Their words can deceive you, but their actions, examined objectively, will tell you everything you need to know about them.

Biden 'Countering Islamophobia' While Incinerating Gaza Is The Most Democrat Thing Ever

In what is arguably the most liberal thing ever to have happened in all of human history, the Biden administration has announced its plans to develop a US National Strategy to Counter Islamophobia even as it helps Israel massacre Muslims by the thousands in Gaza.

"For too long, Muslims in America, and those perceived to be Muslim, such as Arabs and Sikhs, have endured a disproportionate number of hate-fueled attacks and other discriminatory incidents," reads a White House statement on the announcement. "We all mourn the recent barbaric killing of Wadea Al-Fayoume, a 6-year-old Palestinian American Muslim boy, and the brutal attack on his mother in their home outside Chicago."

This comes as the death toll from the US-backed bombing campaign in Gaza nears 10,000, including 3,760 children, in what experts and authorities around the world are describing with increasing frequency as a genocide. If these people were Jewish instead of Muslim, they would not be trapped in a giant concentration camp while the IDF hammers them with a nonstop barrage of military explosives, but because of their ethnicity they are subjected to this horror.

There's a classic meme which makes fun of the way US foreign policy under Democrats is the same murderous foreign policy as it is under Republicans, but with a bunch of woke-sounding bumper stickers slapped on the surface to make it palatable for progressive sensibilities:

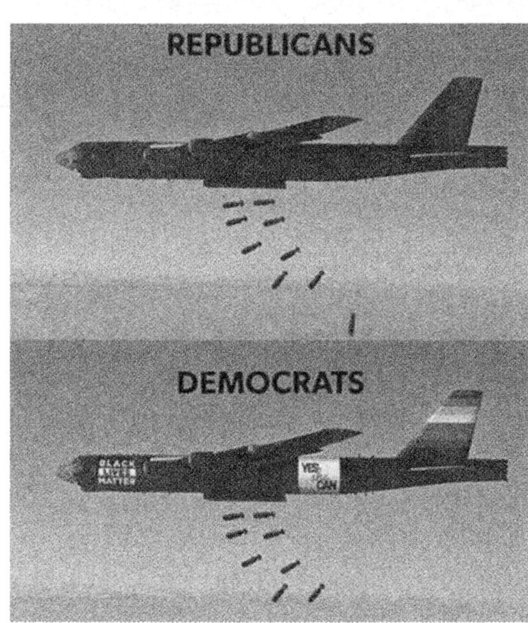

Can you think of a better illustration of the dynamic that's highlighted by this criticism than what we're seeing from the Biden administration today? This is after all the same administration whose Department of Defense recently said they are putting zero limits on what Israel may or may not do with the weapons it's being given by the United States.

"We are not putting any limits on how Israel uses weapons that is provided," Deputy Pentagon Press Secretary Sabrina Singh told the press on Monday. "That is really up to the Israel Defense Force to use in how they are going to conduct their operations. But we're not putting any constraints on that."

As In These Times reports, this same administration is also trying to get permission to conduct arms deals with Israel without congressional supervision, in complete secrecy and without accountability to the voting public.

The US government is every bit as culpable in the massacre of thousands of Muslim children as Israel, because this entire massacre is happening with both its assistance and its express permission. But here is its government pretending to care deeply that one Muslim child was killed by an Islamophobic psycho in America.

This is everything that's disgusting about the Democratic Party. It puts a warm, friendly face on the most murderous and tyrannical power structure on earth, posing as a defender of marginalized groups while dropping bombs on the most marginalized populations on this planet. It selects a high number of women and racially diverse officials for its cabinet positions to convey the illusion that it has transcended the abusive bigotries of the past, while subjecting impoverished brown-skinned foreigners to a nonstop barrage of high tech explosive munitions in massacres that would be the envy of the worst white supremacist imperialists in history.

A much more accurate image for the United States than the one it tries to give itself with its fraudulent progressive virtue signalling would be the one it was given by protesters who interrupted Secretary of State Antony Blinken's testimony before the Senate Appropriations Committee on Tuesday. Demonstrators painted their hands red to show the blood this administration has on its own hands, resulting in viral images of Blinken's face surrounded by bloody hands circulating all over the internet.

That's what the US empire really is. Not the liberal bastion of human rights it presents itself as, but a blood-spattered psychopathic murder machine which maintains its domination of this planet with the nonstop butchery of human beings.

The longer the massacre in Gaza goes on, the more people are catching a glimpse behind the plastic smiley-faced mask of the US empire and seeing the cold-eyed killer underneath.

Featured image by Biden for President (CC BY-NC-SA 2.0 Deed)

We Don't Think Hard Enough About What Bombs Are And What They Do

If I told you that ten thousand people had just been murdered by terrorists in Portland, Oregon—including thousands of children—you would understandably be shocked and horrified. If I told you that they'd all been slashed to pieces by swords, your reaction would be even stronger.

But because the massacre in Gaza is being inflicted upon dark-skinned foreigners in the middle east and is being perpetrated using military explosives instead of blades, most westerners are going about their day without thinking about it much. The same number of people are just as dead as they would have been if they'd been hacked to bits in an American city, but for a westerner it lands different.

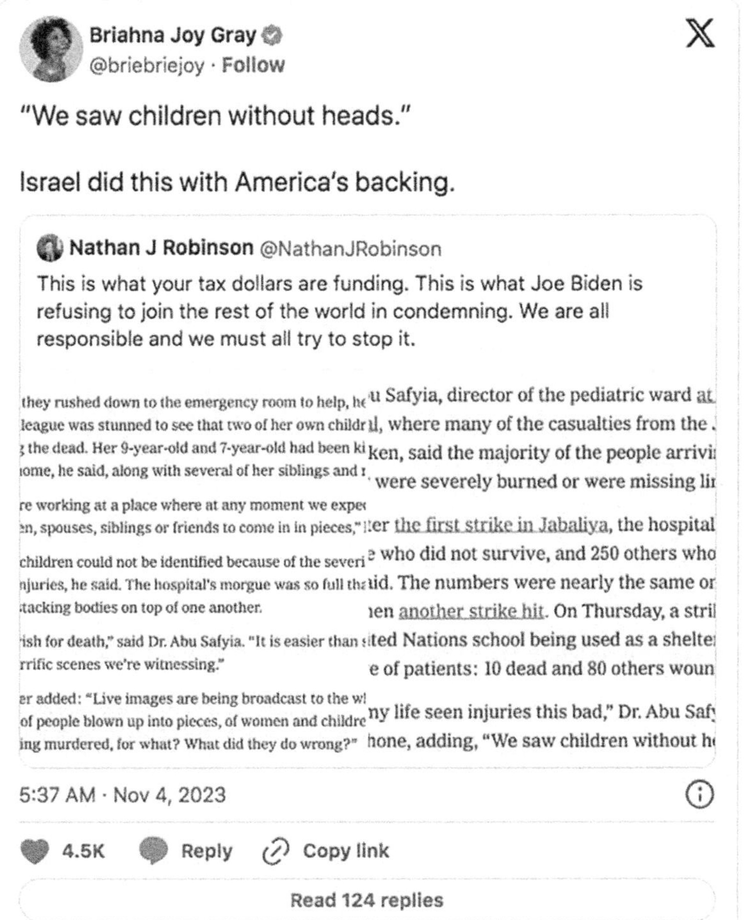

They decapitate. But the public is generally sheltered from the reality of all this by the mass media, who will often just report on "blasts" and "explosions" occurring in empire-targeted territories without even saying who caused them, much less detailing the damage that they inflicted upon human flesh.

The effect these weapons have on the human body is every bit as nightmarish as what you'd see if there was an army of psychopaths going around murdering thousands of civilians with machetes and flamethrowers, but because it's bombs it's not getting the same kind of reaction from the general public.

Part of it is the fact that killing with bombs is something you do from afar. IDF soldiers looks at screens and hit some buttons, and poof, there's a tiny explosion cloud. It's not like looking someone in the eye as you run them through with a blade. It's distant. It's detached from reality.

Another part of it is that with bombs you can say you're not intentionally killing civilians, even while you take actions that you know will kill a lot of civilians like firing military explosives

Because the western empire has been raining military explosives upon the middle east continuously for many years now, westerners have become desensitized to news reports about bombings happening there. If you tell a westerner "There's been a bombing!" with anguish in your voice, they'll immediately assume you're talking about a terrorist attack in New York or London or Paris, not in the middle east. Westerners tend to regard bombings in the middle east as simply the normal state of affairs, as though bombs falling from the sky is just what the weather is like over there.

Westerners aren't the most rigorous thinkers when it comes to the issue of bombs and bombing, and that's entirely by design. An entire propaganda matrix has been constructed by the western empire

to keep us from thinking too hard about what bombs are and what they do, which allows us to preserve our comfortable ideas about our nation and our government that we were taught to believe when we were children.

In Gaza we're getting doctors saying "We saw children without heads" and "Some children could not be identified because of the severity of their injuries", which comes as no surprise to people like myself who spend way too much time looking into this thing online and happen across horrifying footage of this nature on a regular basis.

That is what bombs do to the human body. They rip people to pieces. They squash them with falling buildings. They burn their flesh. They rip their guts out. They blow off body parts.

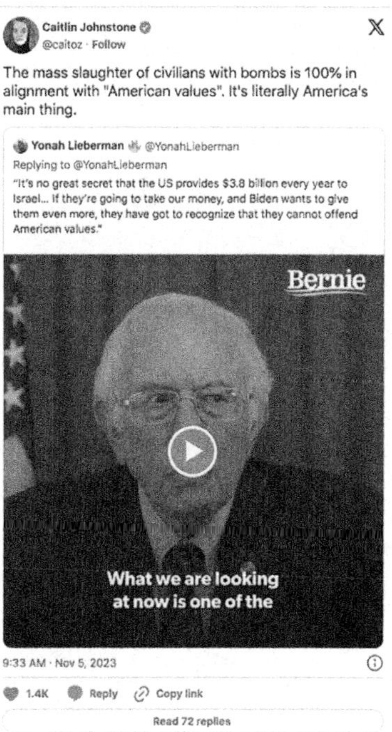

into a densely populated area. Ostensibly it's not that you want to kill civilians, it's that you don't care enough about their lives to refrain from killing them in that instance.

These dynamics help protect the people deploying the bombs from the guilt and trauma of killing large numbers of civilians, which actually makes it easier for them as a collective to kill large numbers of civilians. It lets them feel like they're perpetrating less evil when in reality they are perpetrating more. Which of course benefits the power structure who is ordering them to deploy the bombs.

It's like the invention of execution by firing squad: people in power needed to be able to kill their enemies, so they invented a system wherein multiple executioners fire at the victim simultaneously so that none of them can be sure that they fired the fatal shot. Sometimes one of the guns would even contain a blank cartridge, thereby feeding into the executioners' ability to compartmentalize away from the reality of what they were doing by letting them believe they may not have even fired a bullet. This method of execution allowed for executions to continue in whatever numbers were deemed necessary, without putting a drain on troop morale.

With bombs the same dissociation dynamic is used to a much, much deadlier effect. Both the public and the troops are given the ability to psychologically compartmentalize away from reality and pretend no great evil is being done, the end result of which is to allow much, much more evil to be done. Israeli forces are massacring Gazans no less brutally than if they were mowing them down with machine guns or stabbing them with bayonets, but because the method of massacre lets them dissociate, it allows for a much higher degree of compliance from the troops and a much higher degree of consent from the public.

A tremendous amount of depravity hides behind the completely baseless western delusion that murdering people with bombs is less of an atrocity than murdering them with bullets or blades. In reality, murder is murder and dead is dead. The sooner we can get real with ourselves about that as a civilization, the better.

Featured image via Wikimedia Commons.

The Ten Dumbest Things We're Being Asked To Believe About Israel's War On Gaza

Here are the ten dumbest things we're being asked to believe about Israel's war on Gaza, in no particular order:

1. That Israel had no idea what Hamas was up to prior to October 7, but ever since October 7 has known about every hospital, mosque, school, refugee camp and water tower that Hamas is hiding in.

2. That the blame for all of the deaths caused by Israeli weapons launched by Israel rests solely on Hamas.

3. That Hamas is using "human shields"—meaning Hamas bases are hidden amidst civilian populations—yet Israel is managing to kill thousands of civilians without doing any meaningful damage to Hamas.

4. That it would be perfectly fine to murder children by the thousands even if they were being used as "human shields"—as though resolving a hostage situation by mowing down thousands of child hostages would be regarded as reasonable and acceptable by the public if it happened in our own country.

5. That it is only by pure coincidence that Israel bombing "Hamas targets" in civilian infrastructure and residential buildings just so happens to look exactly the same as what you'd expect to see if Israel was simply bombing civilian infrastructure and residential buildings and lying about its reasons for doing so.

6. That satellite images of entire neighborhoods reduced to rubble in Gaza have been caused by "precision strikes" directed solely at Hamas and have been carried out with the greatest of care for human life, despite Israeli officials openly saying that "the emphasis is on damage and not on accuracy" in this assault and that "Gaza will eventually turn into a city of tents; there will be no buildings."

7. That this bombing campaign has anything to do with freeing Israeli hostages—as though the bombing campaign itself has not killed dozens of hostages, and as though anyone believes Israel would stop bombing Gaza after the hostages are returned.

8. That the only reason anyone could possibly oppose the detonation of thousands of bombs on an open air prison full of children would be if they had very strong and hateful opinions toward the members of the religion of Judaism.

9. That Hamas attacked Israel entirely out of the blue and completely unprovoked, solely because they are evil and hate Jews.

10. That Washington is powerless to stop this genocide that it is directly funding and supplying.

.

There's Only So Much Propaganda Spin You Can Put On The Murder Of Thousands Of Children

The thing is there's only so much propaganda spin you can put on the murder of thousands of children.

With other imperial military actions the propagandists had an easier time spinning things. Oh no those evil communists are taking over South Vietnam, we need to stop them! Oh no Saddam's got WMDs, we need to get him! Oh no Gaddafi's gonna rape and kill all those Libyans, we have a responsibility to protect them!

In Gaza, Israel and its western backers are massacring children by the thousands with a shockingly vicious bombing campaign that is turning entire neighborhoods into gravel. They're raining down military explosives on a giant concentration camp that is densely populated by children.

There's only so much a propagandist can do with that.

They can talk about the killings on October 7 til they're blue in the face, but people are going to object that nothing Hamas did makes it moral or acceptable to murder children by the thousands.

They can say "Israel has a right to defend itself" as much as they want, but people are going to object that murdering children by the thousands is not actually defending anything from anyone.

They can bleat the phrase "human shields" over and over again, but eventually people are going to start saying "Okay but even if they are human shields, could we please stop murdering children by the thousands? I know I wouldn't want my children to be murdered just because they were being used as human shields."

They can say every death is the fault of Hamas, but more and more people are going to start saying "Okay blame whoever you want, but can we please stop murdering children by the thousands right this very instant?"

They can say "Well what do you expect Israel to do?", and people will respond "Stop murdering children by the thousands for starters, please and thank you."

Imagine you're a mass media propagandist trying to frame all this in a positive light. How would you do it? Would you be able to make it believable?

Propagandists are used to having a lot more wiggle room to work with than this. They're used to interfacing with a complex matrix of narrative and manipulating it to distort the public's understanding of what's going on. But raw video footage of a mother clutching the tattered remains of a child is not narrative. Satellite images of powdered city blocks are not narrative. It's just reality. Right there in your face.

Western civilization is dominated by propaganda. The "freedom" and "democracy" we think we have is an illusion that has been carefully cultivated by those who manipulate the way we think, speak, act and vote by mass-scale psychological manipulation—as Chomsky says,

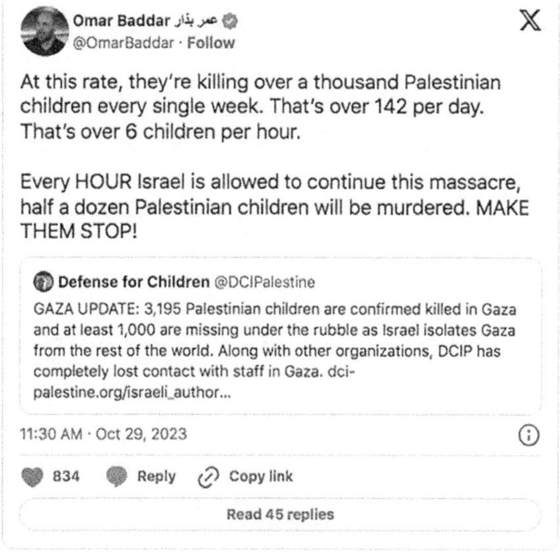

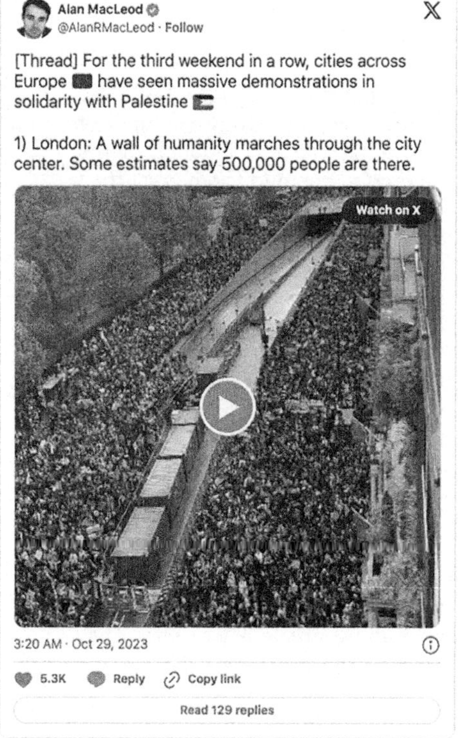

propaganda is to a democracy what the bludgeon is to a totalitarian state. A mind-controlled dystopia is not some dark future that awaits humanity if things go terribly wrong for us; it is already presently the case.

Propagandists are able to control civilization so effectively because they understand that humans are storytelling creatures whose lives are dominated by mental narrative, so if you can control the narratives the humans are telling each other, you can control the humans. A globe-spanning empire centralized around the United States depends heavily on its ability to indoctrinate us with subtle mass media messaging from a very early age.

The Gaza massacre throws a big fat monkey wrench in all that, because the raw data coming out of it is so transparently horrifying that no amount of narrative spin can make it look acceptable. The fact that the US and its allies are helping Israel murder children by the thousands is a giant glitch in the narrative matrix.

The longer this continues, the more people are going to wake up out of the propaganda-induced coma the empire has had them in all their lives. The more people are going to realize that their government is not what it has been pretending to be and the media have not been telling them the truth about the world. As the western empire backs the slaughter of thousands of children, the discrepancies between what the propaganda tells us about our society and what our society actually is are being brightly illuminated.

By murdering thousands of children in Gaza, the empire has exposed its true face in front of everyone. And the people aren't liking what they see.

Eyes are opening everywhere. People are being radicalized in record numbers. The streets are being flooded with protesters. Very inconvenient questions are being asked. Rigorous scrutiny is being applied in places it was seldom applied before. Light is shining in through cracks that weren't there before.

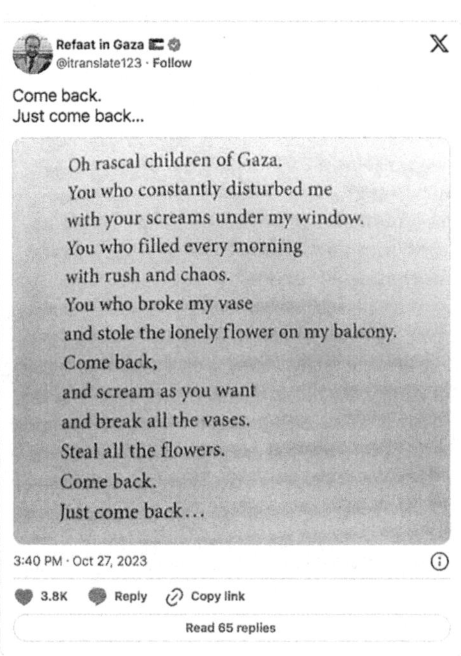

This is all so, so horrible and so, so painful to watch day in and day out. But something is moving underneath it all. Something big. The empire has done irreparable harm to its ability to keep everyone sleeping and complacent going forward. A healthy world may be in our future yet.

Featured image via Socialist Appeal (CC BY 2.0 Deed)

It's Okay To Admit You Were Wrong About Gaza

It's okay to admit you were wrong about this. It's okay to change your mind.

It's okay to admit you reacted inappropriately to the news of what happened on October 7 and advocated some Israeli responses that you should not have advocated.

It's okay to admit that you were wrong to cheer when the bombs started landing on Gaza.

It's okay to admit you were wrong about the longstanding debate over Palestinian rights.

It's okay to admit that you shared some things online that you now regret sharing.

I say this because there are probably a lot of pro-Israel people looking at what's happening in Gaza and starting to feel a bit dissonant about it. Like maybe they're on the wrong side of this thing after all.

And I just want to reassure you that you can change your position on this. It's perfectly fine and normal to do so.

We all make mistakes. We all go through periods where aspects of our worldview are formed by inaccurate information that we were given by others. I know I have. So has everyone else.

It's okay to make mistakes, you just have a responsibility to learn from them and course-correct after you learn that you were mistaken. That's what being a grown-up is all about.

You don't have to make a big public show of admitting you were wrong if you don't want to. You don't even necessarily have to admit it to anyone if this has all been private and internal for you. But you do have

a responsibility to undo any damage you did when you were mistaken about all this.

If you've been cheerleading for the Gaza massacre, you must now begin advocating peace.

If you've been sharing materials supportive of this onslaught, you must start sharing materials which oppose it.

If you taught your children or any young impressionable people who look up to you to support what Israel is doing, you must now teach them the opposite.

If you said things to your family and friends which may have fed into their support for this genocidal slaughter, you must now put forward the opposite stance.

We're all learning as we go. Nobody has it all figured out; those who think they do are typically some of the most insufferable and immature people you'll ever meet. It's fine to make mistakes, and it's fine to turn around once we recognize our error.

It's not a crime to be duped. It's not evil to have been deceived. It would only be morally wrong if you kept persisting in your wrongness after you figured out that you are wrong.

All you can do is your best. But you can't honestly tell yourself that you are doing your best if you've got a nagging feeling inside that you're getting this one wrong and yet do nothing to address it with honesty and integrity.

We can all do something to help bring an end to this horror. None of us can do it single-handedly, but we can all do a little something. Speak out in every medium you have access to, attend demonstrations, talk to your friends and loved ones, and help open as many eyes as possible to the reality of what's happening.

We're all waking up, one pair of eyelids at a time.

Featured image via Wikimedia Commons.

Israel Cut Off Gaza's Communications Because Murderers Don't Like Witnesses

Israeli ground forces have ramped up activities in Gaza in what anonymous US officials are reportedly telling the press is a "rolling start" to the long-anticipated ground invasion.

Israel has also concurrently crippled Gaza's largest telecommunications service, which had been the enclave's last remaining contact with the outside world after Israel knocked out all the others. Humanitarian organizations and mainstream press outlets now say they have lost communication with their contacts in Gaza in a level of information blackout we're unaccustomed to seeing in modern times.

"This information blackout risks providing cover for mass atrocities and contributing to impunity for human rights violations," Human Rights Watch correctly notes.

And I'm going to go ahead and say that's probably not just a convenient coincidence for Israel. A genocidal massacre in total darkness works very much to the advantage of those doing the massacring.

As Israeli siege warfare cuts Gazans off from both electricity and communications, we're seeing the lights go out in Gaza in more ways than one.

The light has been further dimmed by the rampant killing of journalists by the Israeli military. Wikipedia, whose notoriously rigged editing system tends to skew information in the favor of US information interests, still currently lists 17 journalists killed by the IDF in Gaza and another one in southern Lebanon in this current onslaught. NPR lists the numbers a bit higher, while conveniently declining to say who did the killing.

An Al Jazeera reporter named Wael Dahdouh lost his wife, son, daughter and baby grandson to a single Israeli airstrike in Gaza, saying "They're taking their revenge by killing our children!" on the air while kneeling over the body of his dead son. He had reportedly moved them south of Gaza City following an Israeli evacuation order, believing it would keep them safe.

According to Reuters, the IDF is now telling both the Reuters and AFP news agencies that it cannot guarantee the safety of their reporters if they continue operating in the Gaza Strip. After Israel's historically unparalleled assault on journalists these past three weeks, this can only be interpreted as a threat.

As we have discussed previously, Israel has been suffering for years from an increasingly worsening PR crisis as the ability to share and circulate raw video footage of its abuses emerged with the arrival of smartphones and widespread social media access.

During a 2021 video appearance for the International Festival of Whistleblowing, Dissent and Accountability, Israel-based journalist Jonathan Cook made some remarks that I find myself contemplating frequently as Israel scrambles to shut all the lights off in Gaza. Cook described the changes he's seen as smartphones and internet access made Palestinians less dependent on the work of sympathetic western activists and gave them the ability to directly share footage of their own abuse.

Here's a quote:

"Sadly most corporate journalists paid little attention to the work of these activists. In any case, their role was quickly snuffed out. That was partly because Israel learnt that shooting a few of them served as a very effective deterrent, warning others to keep away.

"But it was also because as technology became cheaper and more accessible—eventually ending up in mobile phones that everyone was expected to have—Palestinians could record their own suffering more immediately and without mediation.

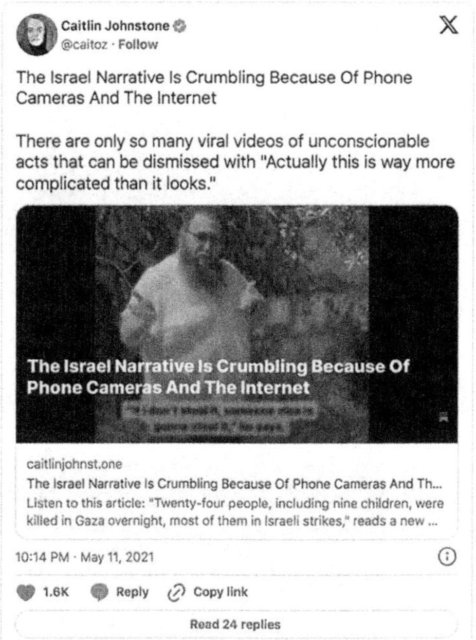

"Israel's dismissal of the early, grainy images of the abuse of Palestinians by soldiers and settlers—as 'Pallywood' (Palestinian Hollywood)—became ever less plausible, even to its own supporters. Soon Palestinians were recording their mistreatment in high definition and posting it directly to YouTube."

Israel is perhaps more acutely aware than any other government on earth of how disadvantageous it is to have your crimes recorded in the light of day and shared with the world. That's why it shut the lights off in Gaza: because murderers don't like witnesses.

Image by Adobe Stock.

As The Lights Go Out In Gaza

In America they killed all the buffalo just to take away food from the natives,
made mountains of their skulls and posed proudly in photos
like they posed proudly in front of burnt bodies after lynchings in the south.

In Australia they stole the brown children and gave them to pale families
and watched their ancient civilization disappear into the toxic fumes of industry
like a sailboat into the mist.

In Israel teenagers play with buttons that cause explosions on screens
and look forward to the end of the Gaza operation
so they can leave and go play better video games.

In Gaza mothers clutch tattered pieces of flesh and clothing to their chests
and scream names that will never again be answered
and call out questions to the heavens that will also go unanswered.

And the ghosts of the buffalo roam through the ruins
looking for their heads
while the people of Gaza comb through the rubble
looking for their dead,
and the rest of us stare at screens and cry like babies
and ask our own unanswered questions
of heavens clouded by the fumes of industry,
vanishing stars above a dying world
as the lights go out in Gaza
one by one.

Image via Wikipedia Commons

The Moral Complexities Of Bombing A Concentration Camp Full Of Children
More Notes From The Edge Of The Narrative Matrix

They're dropping bombs on a concentration camp full of children. THEY'RE DROPPING BOMBS ON A CONCENTRATION CAMP FULL OF CHILDREN.

Not in the past. Right now. They're still doing it. They show no signs of stopping.

No part of opposing this should be remotely controversial.

.

They're dropping bombs on a concentration camp full of kids. Even shitlibs and pseudo-leftists who get every other foreign policy issue wrong are managing to get this one right, it's that obvious. Anyone getting this issue wrong can be permanently dismissed without any real loss.

•

No matter how much you talk about October 7, it will still be a fact that Israel is raining military explosives upon a concentration camp full of children, and that it urgently needs to stop.

No matter how much you talk about how evil and bad Hamas are, it will still be a fact that Israel is raining military explosives upon a concentration camp full of children, and that it urgently needs to stop.

No matter how much you say the words "human shields", it will still be a fact that Israel is raining military explosives upon a concentration camp full of children, and that it urgently needs to stop.

No matter how much you accuse Israel's critics of loving terrorists, it will still be a fact that Israel is raining military explosives upon a concentration camp full of children, and that it urgently needs to stop.

No matter how much you accuse Israel's critics of hating Jews, it will still be a fact that Israel is raining

military explosives upon a concentration camp full of children, and that it urgently needs to stop.

No matter how many words you use or how much narrative spin you try to put on it or how many ad hominems you throw at the people criticizing what Israel is doing, it will still be a fact that Israel is raining military explosives upon a concentration camp full of children, and that it urgently needs to stop.

•

Yeah I'm gonna go ahead and assume that the people arguing that it's necessary to keep dropping military explosives on a giant concentration camp full of children are on the side that will be judged negatively by history.

•

A huge amount of western depravity hides behind the unexamined assumption that killing people with bombs is somehow less evil than killing them with bullets or blades. By waging nonstop foreign bombing campaigns, the west desensitized the public to the reality of what bombs do.

Hamas are in the ambulances. Hamas are in the hospitals. Hamas are underneath the refugee camps. Hamas are behind the children. Maybe they're just massacring civilians.

If a military power was just massacring thousands of civilians and then making up propagandistic lies to cover its massacres, would it look any different from what Israel's actions and statements look like right now?

•

WE are the terrorists.

WE inflict violence and fear on civilian populations to advance political agendas.

WE murder babies.

WE massacre women and children.

The word "terrorism" has no meaning unless you apply it first and foremost to this murderous western civilization.

•

Not since Iraq has the US empire allowed itself to get caught looking this brazenly evil in front of everyone. It's always been the most murderous and depraved power structure on earth, but usually its psychopathy is more hidden and harder for the general public to understand.

And this is like if everyone was watching the Iraq invasion online in real time, with raw footage of all the civilians it's killing flooding their social media feeds 24/7. There's only so much propaganda spin you can put on that.

•

I've seen so many dead kids while gathering information about this massacre. Never seen so many dead kids in my life. I'm already at the point where I see kids around the neighborhood and just feel reflexively grateful that they're standing up and moving and breathing with all their inside parts on the inside, like kids are supposed to be.

•

When the holocaust returned in the 21st century it came denouncing anti-semitism and wearing a Star of David.

•

If you're among the millions of people who are coming to realize that the western political/media class have been lying to you about Israel-Palestine this entire time, you should probably be aware that they've been lying to you about every other foreign conflict as well.

•

Israel created Hamas, in the same way punching someone in the same place repeatedly creates a bruise. If you abuse a population with extreme aggression and deprive them of any peaceful recourse, you're going to see violent factions emerge like a bruise on repeatedly struck flesh.

Believing you can get rid of violent resistance groups with bombs is like believing you can get rid of a bruise by punching it harder, or by switching from punching to hitting it with a bat. The more you abuse the population, the more you're lending cause and legitimacy to the factions which endorse violent resistance to your abuses.

You don't get rid of the bruise with more abuse, you get rid of the bruise by ceasing the abuse and doing everything you can to help heal the wound.

•

The last month has really brought out the best in the best people and the worst in the worst people.

•

I'm sorry if this makes me an evil terrorist-loving baby-raping sieg-heiling Nazi, but in my humble opinion genocidal massacres are bad.

•

Israel and its allies get away with a lot by marketing this as a "war". It's not a war. Israel launches high-tech military explosives at civilian buildings in a huge concentration camp while Hamas fires back with glorified fireworks which do light property damage. That's not a war, it's a massacre.

•

I was upset when I saw that Israel has killed seven thousand people in its Gaza bombing campaign but then a really smart Israel apologist told me Hamas might be exaggerating those numbers and maybe it's more like four thousand, so now I think it's fine.

•

What kind of drooling, knuckle-dragging, tapioca-brained moron can look at the satellite images of the damage caused by Israeli airstrikes and believe Gaza is lying about its death toll?

•

Look it's very simple: if your words say "we're not targeting civilians we're targeting Hamas" but your actions say you're inflicting siege warfare on the civilian population and carpet bombing entire city blocks into rubble, then you're not really targeting Hamas.

•

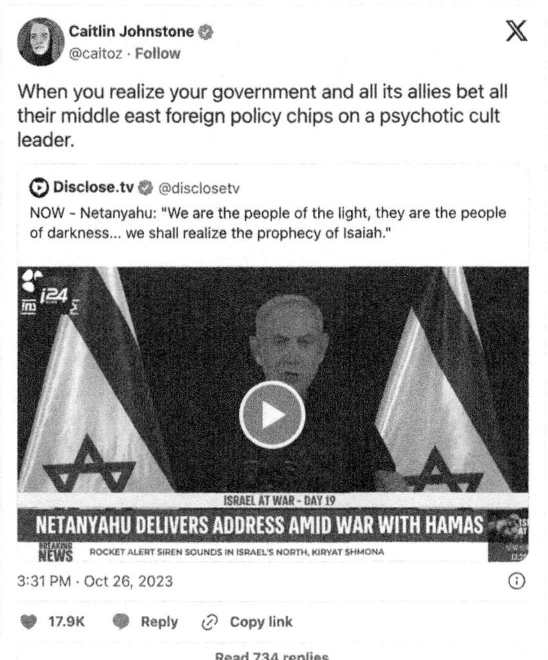

Israel-Palestine is a very complicated, confusing, highly nuanced debate between those who think murdering thousands of children is fine and those who do not.

•

This is a very complicated genocidal massacre. Most complicated genocidal massacre in the history of genocidal massacres. There's two sides to this genocidal massacre. This genocidal massacre requires nuance.

•

Normal person: Israel is killing children by the thousands as we speak

Crazy person: WHY AREN'T YOU CONDEMNING HAMAS??

•

Israel apologists are the worst. The absolute worst. I've sparred with countless political factions over the years, and I've never encountered a group so profoundly morally bankrupt and psychologically malformed. They're so awful that their apologia actually hurts Israel's image. Nothing will reassure you of the moral correctness of your opposition to Israel faster than interacting with Israel apologists online.

•

It keeps surprising me that Israel apologists still expect to be taken seriously. Israel is massacring children by the thousands and turning Gaza into rubble and they still expect you to listen to them receptively when they defend its actions. It's actually starting to get morbidly fascinating.

•

In the old days murderous thugs just grabbed whatever land they wanted and killed anyone who tried to stop them. That still happens today too, but now the thugs have to make up liberal-sounding, sympathy-pulling justifications for it, like "spreading freedom and democracy" or "Israel has a right to defend itself."

Israel has lost the argument. Permanently. There's no coming back from this.

•

I cannot adequately express the immensity of my respect for the many, many, many Jewish voices I've seen taking a firm and forceful stand against the Gaza massacre. I'm just over here getting yelled at by strangers online and I find it pretty intense; you're having much harder arguments with family, with friends, with people you've known your whole lives, about something that probably feels a lot more personal for you. You're out there protesting, taking action and moving the needle, typically with far more skill and incisiveness than anyone else in the world.

Big, big, big-hearted love to all of you. You amaze me.

Featured image via Wikimedia Commons.

The Insane Idea That Nations Get To Do War Crimes Whenever Something Bad Happens To Them

One of the most destructive ideas in modern times is this notion that it's fine and appropriate for governments to act like monsters whenever anything bad happens to their country. We saw it happen with the United States after 9/11, and we're seeing it now with Israel.

Dropping military explosives on children is just as wrong now as it was on October 6th. Wars of aggression were just as wrong on September 12th 2001 as they were on September 10th. But there's this idiotic belief in mainstream culture that a nation experiencing a traumatic event means it gets to go on a murderous rampage until it feels better.

As soon as the Hamas attack occurred we were inundated with messaging from the western political/media class which conveyed the idea that because something bad happened to Israel, Israel now gets to do a little genocide, as a treat. This is stupid nonsense, and should be rejected by all thinking people.

No other aspect of human life works like this. A normal guy isn't permitted to go on a shooting spree at his wife's workplace just because she cheated on him with Kyle from marketing. He's not even allowed to be mean to customers at work or he'll get fired. The rules don't stop applying to normal people just because something bad happened to them; only when we're thinking about the giant power conglomerates known as governments is this sloppy thinking ever taken seriously.

In fact, in other aspects of life we understand that after a traumatic event it's actually important to protect our friends and loved ones from making bad decisions in the emotional heat of the moment. You wouldn't let your sister get an ugly face tattoo after a nasty breakup. If you saw your friend stumbling around with his car keys in one hand and a bottle in the other after losing his job, you wouldn't tell him you stand with him and support whatever it is he's getting ready to do. You'd understand that people can make unwise decisions after something bad happens to them, and you'd do what you can to help steer them away from it.

But when we extend our thinking out to the world's deadliest military forces—precisely the things toward which we should be **most** careful about bad decision-making—all that goes out the window. All of a sudden "You're either with us or against us" is framed as a perfectly sound and reasonable position to have on issues like multiple full-scale ground invasions, and if you don't "Stand with Israel" while it bombs Gaza, Lebanon and Syria that means you're an evil terrorist supporter who probably hates Jews.

The death toll from Israel's bombing campaign in Gaza has already more than doubled the death toll from the Hamas attack, and we can expect it to keep multiplying because there's no meaningful opposition to the bloodshed. The United States, who as an indispensable backer of Israel could end all this with a word, has refused to draw a single red line on what Israel may or may not do if it wishes to retain US support—even its indiscriminate use of white phosphorus, which violates international humanitarian law. War crimes are being committed not just openly but announced in advance as Israel commits itself to the collective punishment of Palestinians with a complete siege of Gaza, and Israel's allies have no objection to this.

And it's pretty bad in the general western public as well. Because of the frenetic propaganda campaign by the western press in the wake of the Hamas attack, a new CNN poll finds that half of Americans have been successfully convinced that because something bad happened to Israel, Israel is "fully justified" in raining hellfire on a giant concentration camp in which half the population are children.

The moments after a scary and traumatizing event are the very moments we should be most vigilant against abuses by the nation affected by it. Instead we're doing the exact opposite as a society and silently agreeing that certain nations get a hall pass on war crimes and mass murder whenever something bad happens to them. At the exact time when the light of wisdom needs to be shining at its very brightest, we're allowing it to be flushed down the toilet.

And now as anti-war voices like Trita Parsi, Branko Marcetic and Connor Echols have noted, we're looking at a conflict that could easily escalate and expand to include other nations in the middle east and the US alliance. All because the world decided that we are now on a temporary holiday away from reason and compassion.

This needs to stop. We need to be thinking rationally not just about the current violence but the factors which led to it. That means taking a full accounting of the apartheid abuses which gave rise to Hamas and the Palestinian resistance, ending those abuses and righting the wrongs. It means negotiations. It means diplomacy. It means reparations. It means making concessions. It means sitting down and talking. It means acknowledging the problem so that it can be fixed.

And all of this can be avoided for as long as Israel and its allies want to strut about huffing about how they have special license to kill Palestinians now because blah blah victim story. At this point in history, just as after 9/11, war looks so very, very easy and peace looks so very, very difficult. But it's at these exact moments that we need to be pushing hardest for peace, because this is when it actually matters.

This is where the rubber meets the road, folks. This is where the real work of creating a healthy world takes place.

Image via Wikimedia Commons

What Would It Look Like If You Were Standing On The Wrong Side Of History?

What would it look like if you were standing on the wrong side of history? If there were a mass atrocity taking place presently which history will end up judging harshly in the future, and you were supporting the wrong side of it, what signs might you expect to see that that's the case?

Well, I imagine you'd probably be seeing terrible news about what's happening coming out every day that under normal circumstances would cause you to cry out in horror, but then you'd be getting a bunch of words and stories from your side explaining why those self-evidently terrible things are actually not what they appear to be.

If you found out thousands of children were being violently killed by your side in this mass atrocity, for example, you'd normally view that information as self-evidently terrible by itself, but then a bunch of narrative framing would come in explaining to you why that information isn't damning for your side. Blame for the deaths of those children would be placed on other parties. If your side was undeniably responsible for their deaths, their deaths would be framed as accidental tragedies which are the unavoidable consequence of military action, and are still indirectly attributable to the actions of the other side.

You'd see the raw data of what's happening, and then an overlay of narrative would be rolled out on top of what you're seeing to alter your perception of that data. And every time, the unaltered data would make your side look bad, while the data filtered through the narrative overlay would make your side look much better.

Over and over again you'd see this take place: information which at a glance makes it look like you're on the wrong side of history, then a deluge of narratives helping you to understand that your eyes deceived you at first actually, and you're on the right side of history after all. Day after day after day this would happen: new terrible information that would normally make you feel bad about your position, followed by narrative framing which makes you feel better about your position.

We may be sure we could expect to see this because we live in a civilization that is dominated by narrative control. Powerful manipulators figured out a long time ago that because human consciousness is dominated by mental stories, if you can control the stories in their heads, you can control the humans. They do this via propaganda and spin, with the wealthiest and most powerful people having the ability to exert the most control over the dominant narratives in our society.

In a sense this leaves us living in two worlds: the real world and the narrative world. The world of unfiltered sensory input controlled by no one, and the world of easily-manipulated mental stories controlled by the rich and powerful. Maturity is waking up out of the narrative world and learning to perceive reality as it's actually happening.

Because the powerful are continuously working to insert narratives about the world into our minds and manipulate our stories about what's happening, it's a safe assumption that if something terrible was being done by powerful people and we were on the wrong side of it, we'd be experiencing a continuous feed of narratives readjusting our perception and understanding of the thing that is happening. This would ensure that we remain supportive of the agendas of those powerful people, even if it leaves us on the wrong side of history.

Anyway, that's just something to keep in mind in case you see anything like that happening in the future. Or who knows? Maybe even in the present.

Featured image via Adobe Stock

Both–Sidesing The Gaza Issue Is A Sign Of Psychological Immaturity

You can't both-sides everything. You can't live your life that way.

Yes it's possible to see both sides of every contentious issue. You're supposed to be able to do that; it's a sign of intellectual maturity. If you can't see both sides of an issue your relationship with abstract concepts is too rigid, and you're probably lacking in empathy. It's just a basic part of growing up to learn how to stand in other people's shoes and see where they're coming from.

But just because you can see both sides doesn't mean you should live your life as though they're both equally true, or as though they both have equal merit. If you want to have a truth-based relationship with reality it's not enough to see both sides; you've got to grapple with it and figure out which side is more truthful, which side has more merit. You're neglecting a whole dimensionality of understanding if you just leave it at "well I can see both sides so I have no responsibility to pick one".

There's a type of personality that has a strong attraction to feeling like it's above the fray; like it's detached from the disputes and dichotomies of the common riff raff, looking down at it all from a lofty place of transcendent understanding. Such people are, without exception, insufferable wankers.

If you want to be an authentic human being, you've got to get down in the muck where the humanness is happening. It's good to understand that all concepts are relative and that none contain absolute truth, but this necessarily means that some concepts are more relatively truthful than others. And we need to be real with ourselves about that.

And if we're honest with ourselves, none of us live our lives as though all things are the same and all concepts are equally true. We don't get up in the morning and pour ourselves a cup of bleach, we pour ourselves some coffee every time. When we want to go to the store we take a specific route to get there, we don't just head out in some random direction and hope for the best. We all make abundant use of relative truths in our day to day lives.

So why should issues like Israel-Palestine be any different? There are a lot of people who've heard both sides of the argument and are content to just leave it there with a shrug, either because they don't want the social backlash that comes from from picking a side, or because they don't want to experience the cognitive discomfort of facing difficult truths and re-orienting their worldview, or because they just enjoy feeling smugly above it all. None of those positions are worthy of respect, in my opinion.

People are dying. Our western governments are helping Israel kill them. This threatens to expand into a much larger war in the middle east, which could end up affecting us and people we know very directly. If you're working hard and raising kids or whatever and have no time to grapple with issues of foreign policy that's one thing, but if you're just psychologically compartmentalizing away from this issue for your own comfort that's quite another. That's just living the life of a coward.

This isn't even that hard. Israel-Palestine is easily the simplest and most straightforward conflict I've had to cover in the time I've been at this commentary gig, and the Gaza massacre in particular is even easier to understand. It doesn't take long to get lucid about this thing.

If you've got the time and the psychological wherewithal to engage this subject then you should do so, and you should do so until you have figured out who is more right and who is more wrong, because this is very important. Get down off that fence and come join the rest of us here in the muck. Come and be an authentic human being.

Featured image via Adobe Stock.

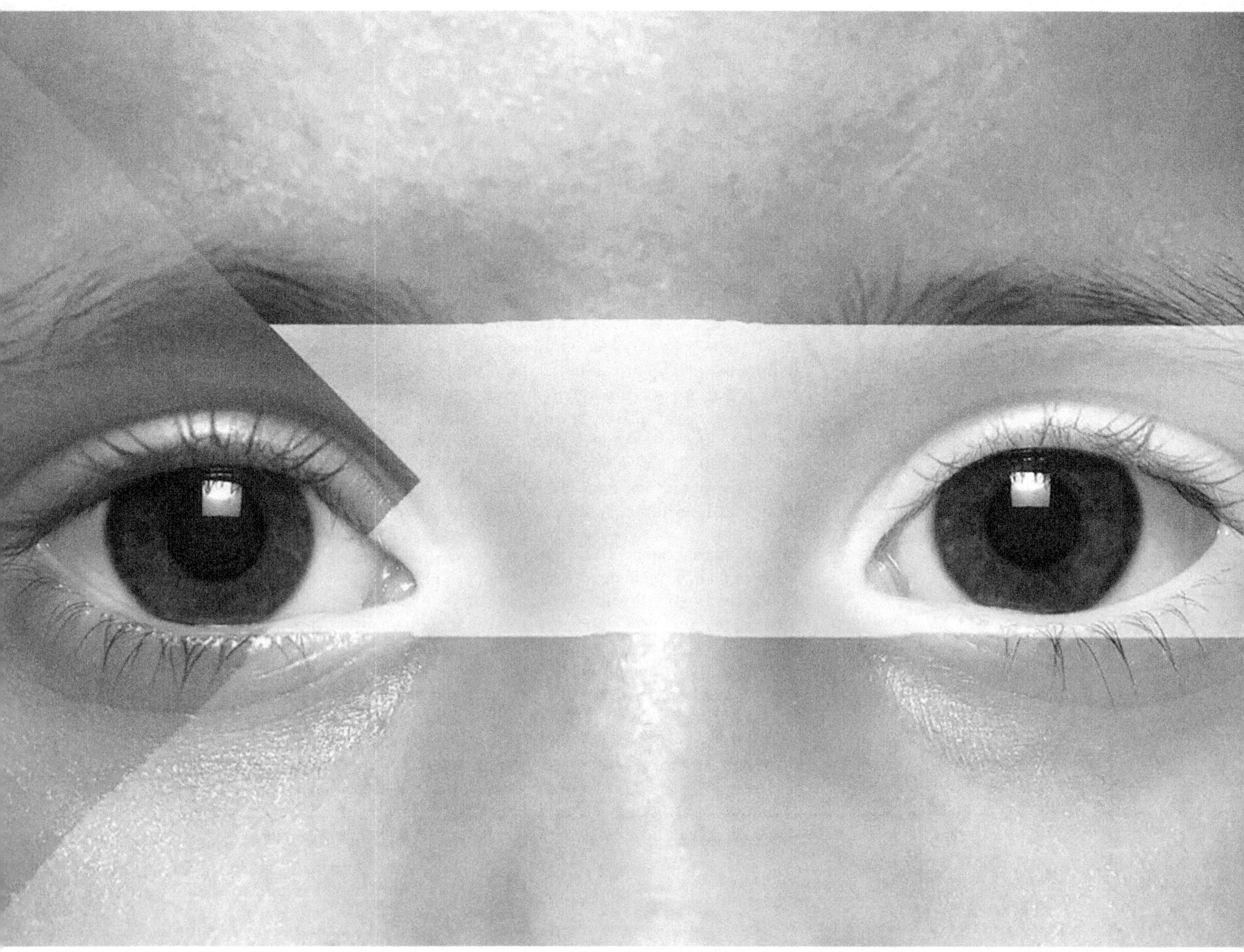

We Keep Our Gaze Fixed On Gaza

I hate every goddamn fucking second of this. I crack jokes here and there to highlight the ridiculousness of the pro-Israel position, but the truth is I've never enjoyed this commentary job of mine less than I've enjoyed it this past month.

Some nights I see dead kids when I close my eyes. There's a phenomenon called the Tetris effect where if you play the classic puzzle video game a lot you start seeing the colorful digital blocks in your mind's eye when the lights are out. For me it's dead Palestinian kids. That's just my life now.

As this horror drags on one seemingly endless day after another I find myself acutely aware not just of the unfathomable suffering in Gaza but of all the other millions of people around the world who are having the same experience I'm having, staring this nightmare dead in the eyes day after day, week after week, unable to look away in good conscience.

I saw an account with the handle @ exomarxi say something on Twitter that I relate to so hard right now: "I don't want to talk about anything else. I don't want to do work. I don't want to do chores or go to the gym or read a book. It reminds me of that feeling you get when a loved one is in intensive care: you feel every fucking second and your adrenaline won't settle and you can't sit still."

It consumes you. It becomes your life. You take short breaks here and there to get some grass under your feet and feel the wind in your hair, but you're only doing it so that you can jump back in and wade through this thing with the attention and reverence it deserves. You can't let yourself burn out, because if you do you won't be able to do your own teeny tiny almost-insignificant little part to help fight this thing in whatever way you can.

But it's more than that really. It's more than the fight. There's also this acute awareness that even if it turns out nothing we do can stop the slaughter in Gaza, it's still important to bear witness to it. You feel a responsibility, just as a human being on this planet, to keep your gaze fixed on what's happening and to not look away.

It feels... sacred. The responsibility, I mean. I don't even really know what that word means, but that's the only word that clicks into place and feels appropriate when I describe this responsibility to witness the mass atrocity in Gaza with eyes wide open. It's a sacred duty that we have to our species. To the universe even, maybe.

It could be as simple as an urge to resist the calls from the powerful to look away. All the world's most powerful institutions want us to avert our gaze, to scroll on, to dissociate, to take our attention elsewhere. We're all engaging in a very simple act of defiance by bringing attention and awareness to the very last thing the powerful want our attention and awareness on, one pair of eyes at a time.

So we keep our gaze fixed on Gaza. No matter how much it hurts. No matter how horrifying it gets. No matter how much we cry. No matter how often we slump over and feel like we can't do it anymore. We keep our gaze fixed on Gaza. Because what else can we do? Nothing else feels right. Nothing else feels responsible.

I don't know when this will end, or why. I don't know if it will end because all the opposition made it politically untenable for Israel and its powerful western allies to continue, or because there was nothing left to bomb, or no one left to kill. It kind of feels like that's none of my business. Because I'm in this with all of me no matter what. Come what may. My life doesn't really feel like it belongs to me anymore.

Anyways that's enough of that for the time being. Mainly I just wanted to let everyone who's holding this same vigil know that I see you, and I appreciate you, and I value you, and you're not alone, and you never will be. I raise my glass to you beautiful, beautiful souls.

Thank you so much for bearing witness.

Featured image via Adobe Stock.

On Gaza And Human Consciousness

It gets harder and harder for the imperial propagandists to frame empire-targeted powers like Hamas as Evil Villains who are simply Evil because they are Evil. As our society gains a better and better collective understanding of psychology and trauma and why individuals do what they do, fewer and fewer people are swallowing such infantile propagandistic frameworks. When something scary and traumatizing happens, more and more people are beginning to ask, "Why? Why did that happen? What were the antecedents which led those people to do what they did?"

When people start asking such questions, answers are revealed which are very inconvenient for the information interests of the western empire. Oh it turns out Israel is an abusive apartheid state and Gaza is a giant concentration camp where Palestinians are deprived of basic human needs. Oh it turns out NATO was amassing war machinery near Russia's border in ways the United States would never in a million years permit near its own borders. Oh it turns out western powers were funneling weapons to murderous extremist groups in Syria with the goal of ousting Assad and installing a puppet regime in Damascus.

More and more people understand that nobody is just plain evil because they are evil; if they're doing something violent and scary, it's a safe bet that something violent and scary was done to them, either immediately before or in their formative years. You see this expanding awareness manifest today in popular movies and shows with the rise of the anti-hero and complex villains with traumatic pasts that you can understand and sympathize with. Modern storytelling has largely abandoned the Virtuous Protagonist vs Villainous Antagonist model, simply because audiences are too conscious to buy it anymore. It loses their interest and attention.

And of course this expanded awareness extends to Israel as well. A people who had just suffered an unfathomable collective trauma were told they have a place that they can call their own in the Holy Land where they can feel safe, and then we saw the kind of violence and abuse we'd expect to see from a highly traumatized population who suddenly had power over the indigenous people who were living there previously. That trauma went into the psyches of the Palestinians, who sometimes do things only highly traumatized people would do.

And round and round it goes.

Really we're all just lost little kids stumbling around from jump scare to jump scare in a frightening world that we do not understand. Some of us are better at faking self-assuredness than others, but really none of us know what this big mysterious world is all about and we only do what we do because we are whipped around by forces within ourselves we can't really see, which were put there when we were too young to understand the trauma that was happening to us.

That's all this really is. It comes out in some ugly, horrifying ways, like what we're seeing in Gaza right now, but underneath it all it's ultimately just scared little kids frozen in grown adult bodies trying to feel like they have a little bit of control in this wild chaotic world so they maybe won't get hurt and scared again.

It comes out in some dark, dark ways and leads our species down some dark, dark paths. It might even get us all killed in a nuclear holocaust one day. But underneath it all we were always just a bunch of scared little primates, getting thrown around by psychological forces we hadn't made conscious in a world our newly evolved brains aren't equipped to comprehend.

I don't know where our strange adventure is taking us or what we'll endure on the remainder of our winding road together. But there does seem to be a light growing, even amid all the violence and the screams. Maybe we'll wake up one day and stop acting out these terrible patterns. Maybe we'll wake up one day and build a healthy world.

Featured image via Adobe Stock.

If Israel Stops Murdering Thousands Of Children, The Bad Guys Might Win
Notes From The Edge Of The Narrative Matrix

You see kids, Israel needs to keep dropping bombs on buildings full of children and targeting civilians with siege warfare and murdering Palestinians in the West Bank and censoring the media and arresting dissidents and killing journalists, because if it doesn't, the bad guys will win.

No no you don't understand: if Israel stops killing children by the thousands in its relentless bombing campaign, the nation could be taken over by murderous terrorists.

Normal person: It's wrong to kill children by the thousands by dropping military explosives on the places where they are known to be located.

Crazy person: Oh so you're saying you love Hamas and you want them to kill every Jew in the world???

·

Normal person: It's wrong to drop bombs on buildings full of children and it needs to stop right now.

Crazy person: BUT A BAD THING HAPPENED TWO WEEKS AGO

·

One of the dumbest things Israel apologists ask us to believe is this bizarre narrative that Hamas bears 100 percent of the responsibility for the children killed by Israeli bombs, and Israel bears zero percent of the responsibility. It's just self-evidently moronic and nonsensical.

And the thing about this framing is there's no upper limit on it. If Israel kills 10,000 children, Hamas killed 10,000 children. If Israel kills 100,000 children, then Hamas killed 100,000 children. If Israel exterminates all the Palestinians, then Hamas exterminated all the Palestinians.

It's plainly absurd.

·

Israel-Palestine is not complicated, it only looks complicated after you add in all the freakish mental contortions Israel's apologists ask you to perform to make it look like its self-evidently indefensible abuses are justifiable.

·

The thing about Israel apologists who say Israel needs to go scorched earth on Gaza or else there'll be another Hamas attack is that, in the sense that they mean it, they're correct. Because they have already ruled out the option of rolling back the many Israeli abuses which led to the rise of Hamas and the attack on October 7, it is a safe bet that if they agreed to a ceasefire right now and returned to the abusive status quo which provoked the attack it would only be a matter of time before Gazans launched another one. So, from within that framework, the only other option is to kill and kill and kill and destroy and destroy and destroy until Gaza can pose no further threat.

The problem, of course, is that their framework is bullshit. The obvious other option is to move toward peace and reconciliation and right all the wrongs which gave rise to the attack on October 7, which would mean a one-state or two-state solution that Palestinians are happy with instead of the status quo of apartheid and tyranny and ghettos and a giant concentration camp of profound human suffering. That would allow the possibility of a ceasefire without the need for continued Palestinian resistance.

But Israel is unwilling to do this because it would mean ceding a bunch of land or ending Israel's existence as a Jewish ethnostate, so that option is framed as unthinkable nonsense instead of the glaringly obvious fix for this problem that it plainly is. Murdering children by the thousands and carpet bombing Gaza is seen as preferable to the measures that would be necessary to achieve a lasting peace.

·

Officially Israel has three options:

1. Make huge compromises and right all wrongs so the Palestinian resistance has no further reason to exist,

2. Return to the status quo and accept that there will be more attacks in the future, or

3. Go scorched earth genocide on Gaza.

A hidden fourth option which nobody wants to talk about would be to address the uncomfortable fact that Israeli intelligence probably allowed the Hamas attack to happen. It seems highly unlikely that Hamas spent two years coordinating and openly training for an attack of unprecedented scale and sophistication involving motorboats, drones and motorized paragliders in an enclosed area the size of Philadelphia which also happens to be one of the most spied-on places on earth, and that the attack was carried out so successfully even Hamas was surprised at how many Israelis they were able to kill and capture because it went completely undetected by Israeli intelligence those entire two years despite being warned by Egyptian intelligence that an attack was coming, and despite the fact that US intelligence was aware of unusual activity by Hamas on October 6.

If Israel got real with itself and investigated and found that officials in Israeli intelligence kept operatives looking the other way to allow the October 7 attack to occur, then simply acknowledging this and taking steps to ensure that it never happens again would be enough to feel secure that Israel won't suffer any more attacks of that scale, because Israeli intelligence can indeed prevent them from happening. The premise that Hamas needs to be eliminated to prevent such attacks would be proven false.

This is perhaps the least likely of all possible options, though, because the internal political fallout that would occur when the Israeli public learns their nation's intelligence services sacrificed massive numbers of their own citizens to advance a pre-existing agenda would collapse the entire national order.

•

Israel apologists are like, "All you goddamn anti-semitic terrorist lovers just don't get it: if Israel doesn't go full scorched earth and completely obliterate Hamas right now, what's to stop another massive Hamas attack from being intentionally allowed to happen by Israeli intelligence?"

•

Funny how empire simps spent the last seven years screaming the word "whataboutism" and saying it's evil, and now their response to all criticisms of Israel is "what about what Hamas did" and "what about those other countries who do bad things".

•

Westerners who didn't already know about Israel's criminality have been learning that Israel

Routinely bombs hospitals, churches and mosques

Constantly lies and circulates disinformation

Is fine with killing children by the thousands

Sees Palestinians as sub-human

We're fast approaching the point where the emotional heat of October 7 wears off and people start looking at Israel's actions more rationally, after which point they'll look over and just see Israel murdering children by the thousands and reducing Gaza to rubble for no legitimate reason.

•

The premise behind this current onslaught and those which preceded it is that you can bomb people into consenting to oppression and apartheid. That you can abuse them into accepting abuse. The whole entire argument is that if you bomb and shoot and teargas and beat and imprison enough Palestinians with enough aggression, eventually they will see the error of their ways and accept the status quo you are trying to impose upon them.

This is of course stupid, and it is of course a lie. The idea was never really to abuse Palestinians into accepting abuse, that's just the cover story; the real goal has always been to abuse them to the point where you can justify eliminating them. To push an inconvenient people into an impossible corner and then when they push back hard enough say "Well, we did all we can and we learned you just can't help these savages. They're going to have to go."

•

I can't stop tripping on how fast the west moved from arming and applauding Nazis to backing an actual genocide.

•

Israel: Our intelligence services had no idea Hamas was planning its attack on October 7.

Also Israel: Here's an audio clip from our intelligence archives of Hamas fighters talking to each other.

If I had not bombed a hospital, I personally would refrain from publishing an easily debunked audio file of me talking to myself pretending to be two different guys telling each other Caitlin definitely didn't bomb the hospital.

•

My favorite kooky conspiracy theory is the one where Hamas spent two years coordinating and training for an attack of unprecedented scale and sophistication involving motorboats, drones and motorized paragliders in an enclosed area the size of Philadelphia which also happens to be one of the most spied-on places on earth, and this conspiracy by Hamas was carried out so successfully that even Hamas was surprised at how many Israelis they were able to kill and capture, because their conspiring went completely undetected by Israeli intelligence those entire two years despite being warned by Egyptian intelligence that an attack was coming, and despite the fact that US intelligence was aware of unusual activity by Hamas on October 6.

•

Israel's being so obvious about wanting to do another land grab. The solution is always to move Gazans off the land they're on to somewhere else. It's like a guy at a nightclub pushing you and pushing you to drink a drink he handed you; at a certain point you realize he's probably not really interested in making sure you have enough to drink.

•

"Honey I took down the Ukraine flag to put up the Israeli flag, where should I put it?"

"Bottom drawer."

"The one with the Black Lives Matter flag?"

"Yeah, just throw it on top."

"It doesn't fit, there's too many other flags in there."

"Throw out the MeToo one then."

"Not the Pride one?"

"Whatever, I don't care."

•

I used to think it's bad to detonate military explosives in buildings full of children but then a really smart Israel apologist called me an anti-semite so now I think it's good.

•

Israel apologists are seriously asking you to believe that the only reason anyone could possibly object to a government dropping military explosives on children is that they have extremely negative opinions about adherents to the religion of Judaism.

"I see you think it's wrong to launch missiles into locations known to be packed with children. The only possible explanation for this is that you have a deep and profound hatred for the members of a small Abrahamic religion."

Saying it's anti-semitic to oppose bombing areas full of children is itself anti-semitic blood libel. That's what you are doing when you associate the murder of children with some innate quality in Jewish people instead of the violence of a specific nation's government.

•

Israel apologists who are getting frustrated that nobody's buying their "criticism of Israel is anti-semitic" routine anymore can thank the smear campaign against Jeremy Corbyn a few years ago. It opened a lot of eyes to how cynically that accusation is used.

•

I'm always getting people calling me a Hamas supporter and saying I'm "spreading terrorist propaganda" these last two weeks. Before that I was a Chinese agent who was "spreading CCP propaganda". Before that I was a Russian troll who was "spreading Kremlin propaganda". I'm never just a person on the internet sharing her opinions, because any opinions which go against US information interests are "propaganda".

At a certain point all the empire simp ad hominems all start sounding the same. These dopes just have no argument and can't think anything they weren't told to think.

I'm not a celebrity. I have no platform. I use the same free blogging and social media sites everyone else uses. People just share my criticisms of the world's most powerful and destructive power structure because they like what I have to say, and empire simps can't handle it.

Featured image via Adobe Stock.

How Much Killing Is Enough Killing?

Israel has killed multiple times as many people since October 7 as were killed on October 7, has caused many times more destruction since October 7 than was caused on October 7, and has inflicted many times more pain and suffering since October 7 than was inflicted on October 7.

Even if you completely ignore the power dynamics and abuses which led to the Hamas attack and just look impartially at the raw data, it's an easily quantifiable fact that what Israel has done since October 7 is worse than what Hamas did on October 7. While there is a huge taboo against saying this publicly, it's not seriously debatable. The only way to make it seem otherwise would be to see Palestinian lives as worth less than Israeli lives, which is not a position that deserves to be taken seriously.

But that isn't the foremost objective fact separating the death and destruction on October 7 from all the death and destruction that's happened since. The foremost objective fact separating the death and destruction on October 7 from the death and destruction that's happened since is that October 7 already happened, while the Gaza massacre is still ongoing and can be stopped.

Everything that happened on October 7 is in the past. It's done. No matter how many bombs the IDF drops, no matter how many civilians in Gaza are killed, no matter how many buildings are smashed to rocks and powder, no matter how much propaganda the western media churn out, it won't bring one single Israeli who died on October 7 back to life.

Nothing about October 7 can be changed. It's in the past. We have no access to it. But what can be changed is the decision to keep killing civilians by the thousands with a relentless barrage of military explosives and strangling them to death with siege warfare for something they did not do.

At any time Israel could stop turning entire city blocks into rubble and adding to the thousands of children who've been killed, but they don't. It's still happening. Every hour this goes on is another decision made by the Israeli government to keep it going, and every hour it keeps going is more death and human misery in Gaza.

And at a certain point there's a very important question that will need to be answered, and that question is this: how much is enough?

How much killing is enough killing? How many civilians need to die before we can draw a line under this one?

How high does the pile of mutilated and dismembered children need to be before it's high enough? Give me a specific height please, in meters or in yards.

It's an answer we're going to come to one way or another. At some point we're going to reach the end of the killing, either because some sliver of conscience awakened in the powers perpetrating and facilitating it, or because it became politically inconvenient to continue, or because some meaningless and arbitrary goal was declared to have been met, or because the killers felt satiated by the amount of killing they'd done, or because there was no one left to kill.

So we may as well begin chewing on that question right now so we can get settle on a number as soon as possible. How much is enough? It's a question that demands an answer. And the answer we come to collectively will say a lot about our species, and about where it is headed.

Featured image via Adobe Stock.

The Wise And Brilliant Israel Apologist

I used to be pro-Palestinian, you know. I thought Israel was wrong for carpet bombing Gaza and using siege warfare on civilians.

But then I ran into a very wise Israel apologist who changed my way of looking at things forever.

I was walking down the street and I saw him leaning against a lamp post, smoking a pipe as wise men do.

"Your shirt says Free Palestine," he said from behind a plume of smoke.

"Yep!" I replied.

"So I guess that means you love Hamas then?" spake he.

I stopped in my tracks. I'd never thought of it that way before.

Could it be? Could my opposition to murdering civilians really be indicative of a deep affection for a Gazan militant group? Maybe I really did love Hamas and think everything it did on October 7 was great and wonderful?

"Is this really how I want to live my life?" I thought to myself.

"I—I—I..." I said out loud.

"Or perhaps," he said with a raised eyebrow, "you just HATE JEWS??"

I fell to my knees.

Oh my God. He really had a point. What possible reason could anyone have for opposing military explosives being dropped on buildings full of children besides a seething lifelong hatred of adherents to the religion of Judaism? How could anyone possibly oppose siege warfare tactics which cut off civilians from food and water and electricity and fuel and medical supplies unless they harbored dangerously negative opinions about members of a small Abrahamic faith?

"Who... who are you?" I asked.

"That's of no consequence," he said, casually blowing a smoke ring through another larger smoke ring.

"But... but the children," I stammered as my entire worldview crumbled before my eyes. "The civilians! They're dying! Isn't it bad that they're dying?"

And then he delivered the coup de grâce.

"Have you considered," he said before a pregnant pause, "... that all of those deaths are the fault of Hamas?"

It was like a 50 megaton nuclear explosion went off inside my brain.

I fell flat on my back. The world was spinning. A trickle of blood ran down into my hair from my ear.

I felt all the anti-colonialism leaving my body. I suddenly could no longer remember why I thought it was bad to rain down military explosives on a densely populated concentration camp.

Everything went black.

When I finally came to, the mysterious stranger was gone. But his wisdom and profound insights into Israel and Gaza will always live on in my heart.

Featured image via Adobe Stock.

Getting Called A Nazi For Opposing A Genocide
More Notes From The Edge Of The Narrative Matrix

It's the most 2020s thing in the world that there's an active genocide currently underway and it's the people who oppose it who are being called Nazis.

•

Gaza isn't one of those issues where you have to respect the other side's opinions. Supporting a genocidal massacre is not an acceptable opinion for anyone to have. This is worth hurting people's feelings over. Worth losing friends over. Worth disrupting Thanksgiving dinner over.

•

Anyone who looks at these numbers and still opposes a ceasefire is saying something significant about who they are as a person. They're saying their conscience has not formed properly. That they never developed into mature adults. That they have wasted their time on this planet.

•

I've been writing for years about the murderous foreign policy of the US and its sidekicks Australia and the UK, but when Israel starts massacring children by the thousands its apologists tell me I've got a hateful fixation on Israel for writing about it. These people are ridiculous, and do not deserve to be taken seriously.

•

BREAKING: Sources say some Hamas fighters may have been injured in crossfire from Israeli airstrikes on children and civilian infrastructure.

•

Ah shit you guys we gotta let Israel keep murdering thousands of kids, turns out if you squint really hard at the phrase "from the river to the sea" the words transform into "genocide the Jews".

•

It is right to call for the abolishment of the murderous apartheid ethnostate of Israel, in the same way it was right to call for the end of apartheid South Africa. Only by the most determined mental gymnastics does calling for all Palestinians to be freed from apartheid, murder and abuse due to their ethnicity sound like a call for the genocide of Jews.

•

A state whose existence requires the mass murder of children every few years is not a state that should continue to exist.

•

It's a crazy coincidence how Israel bombing Hamas in ambulances, hospitals, mosques, schools, refugee camps, water towers and buildings full of children looks exactly the same as what it would look like if Israel was just massacring civilians with bombs.

•

This belief that it's fine and good for a government to keep massacring children by the thousands until its enemies give it what it wants is just about the most evil position you can possibly imagine anyone espousing. And it's very, very mainstream among Israel apologists.

•

You don't understand man, Hamas uses human shields. Really really advanced human shields, the kind where there aren't even any Hamas members anywhere near them. It's just 100% human shield with 0% combatant, the most secure kind of shield there is.

•

Everyone who advocates de-escalation and ceasefire is always accused of treacherous loyalism to the other side. Always, always, always. It happened with Ukraine, and it's happening again with Gaza.

Ever since the war in Ukraine started those of us who called for peace talks were accused of being Putin lovers and Russian agents. Almost two years and mountains of human corpses later and the US is starting to push Kyiv to accept a peace deal that will almost certainly be worse than the one that was on offer at the beginning of the conflict.

All that death and destruction, for absolutely nothing. The only ones who benefitted from that nightmare were the war profiteers who raked in vast fortunes and the empire managers who used it to advance their geostrategic agendas in Eurasia. Those of us who called for peace negotiations were objectively correct, and those who shouted us down and accused us of treasonous Kremlin loyalism were objectively wrong.

Those calling you an anti-semitic baby-cooking terrorist lover for supporting a ceasefire are wrong in exactly the same way for exactly the same reasons. All the arguments being made against peace right now will only end up serving the

The New York Times

It is not clear how effective Israel's campaign against Hamas has been. One senior U.S. defense official, who spoke on condition of anonymity to discuss sensitive details, said the operations so far have not come close to destroying Hamas's senior and middle leadership ranks. Other U.S. officials said Hamas is not analogous to Al Qaeda or the Islamic State, and has a far deeper bench of experienced midlevel military leaders, making it hard to assess the impact of killing any individual commander.

rich and powerful, at the cost of unfathomable oceans of human suffering.

You get peace by making peace. That's how you do it. You stop shooting, you sit down, you have conversations and you make deals. The deals won't feel perfect, because they won't be, but they will be better than slaughtering children by the thousands for no justifiable reason and killing off parts of our own humanity in the process. You set your intention toward peace and harmony, and you start walking in that direction, one step at a time.

It really is that simple. Anyone who tells you otherwise is lying for the benefit of the rich and powerful.

•

I feel sorry for Zelensky. The US abandoning your country for Israel is like your husband leaving you for his first wife.

Top reasons Americans are supporting the Gaza massacre right now:

1. Their favorite right wing pundits told them to.

2. They hate Muslims.

3. They want a biblical prophecy to be fulfilled in which Jesus comes back and casts non-Christians into eternal hellfire.

4. Dopey partisan culture war bullshit.

5. The news media lied to them.

•

"Israel has a right to defend itself" means "Genocide all non-Zionists." If pro-Israel people get to decide that "From the river to the sea, Palestine will be free" is a call to genocide Jews, then it's only fair that pro-Palestine people get to decide what pro-Israel people's slogans mean as well.

•

Person in 1940: Nazi Germany must end.

Other person in 1940: SO YOU'RE SAYING YOU WANT TO GENOCIDE THE GERMANS??

•

Schrödinger's ethnostate: simultaneously (A) the only place in the world where Jews can exist safely and (B) a poor little victim whose inhabitants are under constant threat from violent militants and hostile neighboring nations.

•

The question "How can Israel destroy Hamas if there's a ceasefire?" is infinitely less relevant and interesting than the question "How can Israel continue to exist as a Zionist ethnostate without apartheid and abuse and nonstop murder and endless warfare?"

•

More than 20 House Democrats joined Republicans in voting to censure Palestinian-American congresswoman Rashida Tlaib on Tuesday for her comments supporting Palestinians against Israel's murderous assault on Gaza.

Democrats were happy to have a Palestinian woman in congress until they found out she was the "Palestinians are human beings" kind of Palestinian and not the "Look how diverse and inclusive Democrats are" kind.

They're like, "I was fine with the Palestinian woman until she started supporting the Palestinians. Did nobody tell her that her only job is to quietly pose for Instagram selfies with Nancy Pelosi?"

·

White House spokesman John Kirby has confirmed that the Biden administration is still drawing zero red lines with how Israel is permitted to use US-supplied weapons in Gaza. Asked by the press on Tuesday if it is still the case that "the administration is not drawing any red lines for Israel" despite the soaring death toll in Gaza, Kirby replied, "That is still the case."

This is the same Biden administration who just days ago was telling the press that it is powerless to stop Israel from massacring civilians in Gaza, now telling us that they've made literally no effort to stop Israel from massacring civilians. It's a blatant case of "We've tried nothing and we're all out of ideas."

·

It's not just the Israeli state that has proven it needs to be dismantled, it's the entire US-centralized western empire. The whole giant power structure has got to go.

Israel has once again released an audio clip of what it claims is an intercepted Hamas phone call in order to rebuff accusations of war crimes, this time allegedly featuring a Hamas fighter boasting about how many ambulances he's able to use for transportation in response to criticisms of a deadly Israeli airstrike on an ambulance convoy.

The last time Israel released such an audio file in an attempt to exonerate itself, language experts cited by the UK's Channel 4 News said the clip was not credible due to the " language, accent, dialect, syntax and tone" in the clip, and audio analysts with an organization called Earshot "found that this recording was manipulated and cannot be used as a credible source of evidence."

This is also the very same government which claims its intelligence agencies had no idea what Hamas was up to in the lead-up to the October 7 attacks, now claiming it is constantly intercepting Hamas communications and has a whole archive of them it can access whenever it needs to exonerate itself from accusations of war crimes. Bit odd, that.

·

Featured image via Adobe Stock.

A True Story About Israel And Palestine

A husband and a wife were standing on top of a man one day drinking tea.

"Do we still have milk?" asked the wife.

"Yeah, like half a carton," said the husband.

"HELP!" screamed the man.

"Oh well that's good," said the wife. "I was thinking I might have another cup of tea after this one."

"Hmm, well maybe I'll join you," said the husband.

"Good tea," said the wife.

"YOU'RE CRUSHING ME!" yelled the man.

"Think it'll rain today?" the husband asked.

"Oh maybe," answered the wife. "Looks a little gray out, doesn't it?"

"I CAN'T BREATHE!" the man shouted. "I'M DYING!"

"I'll hold off on watering the garden then," said the husband.

"That's probably a good—ahhh!" screamed the wife.

Her ankle was bleeding. The man they were standing on had slashed her with a piece of glass he'd found on the ground.

"What? What happened?"

"HE CUT ME!"

"You bastard! I'll kill you!"

They both began angrily stomping on the man and jumping up and down on him.

"Monster! Filth!"

"I'll teach you to attack us!"

Other people standing around them took notice of the commotion.

"What happened?" someone asked. "What's this all about?"

"We were just standing there minding our own business and this monster attacked us, completely unprovoked!" the husband said, kicking the man in the groin.

"We were just peacefully drinking our tea and going about our lives," sobbed the wife while stomping on the man's throat. "No one could have seen this coming!"

"Oh no!" cried the others. "We stand with you!"

"Get him! Kick him harder!" someone yelled.

A large muscled man ran over to them.

"Here are a bunch of weapons," he said. "You make that bastard pay!"

The husband and the wife began stabbing and slashing the man with the weapons. They stabbed him and stabbed him and slashed him and slashed him, furiously taking revenge on his flesh.

"What did we ever do to you??" they screamed at him.

They kept hacking and slashing, gouging and severing. Blood spurting everywhere. Screams filling the air.

After a while, the faces of the onlookers started to change.

"Uhh, how long are you going to keep laying into him like that?" someone asked.

"UNTIL HE'S GONE!" they screamed.

They kept chopping away.

"Uhhh, I think maybe he's learned his lesson?" someone said tentatively.

"Yeah, perhaps it's getting time to think about laying down the weapons," added someone else.

"What else do you expect us to do?" said the husband. "These savages only understand violence!"

They continued their onslaught while the onlookers grew more and more uncomfortable.

A woman broke down in tears.

One of the men ran away and vomited.

"Oh god," someone said. "What have we done?"

I don't know what happened after that, yet.

Featured image via Adobe Stock.

All Israel Apologists Have Are Ad Hominem Attacks

The Washington Post has a new article out explaining why it and other mainstream media outlets have been citing the Gaza Health Ministry as a source on the daily death toll from Israel's ongoing bombing campaign, noting that the ministry has an established track record of reporting such deaths truthfully and accurately.

"Everyone uses the figures from the Gaza Health Ministry because those are generally proven to be reliable," Human Rights Watch's Omar Shakir told the Post. "In the times in which we have done our own verification of numbers for particular strikes, I'm not aware of any time which there's been some major discrepancy."

This point is inconvenient for Israel apologists—including the president of the United States—who've been suggesting in recent days that the Gaza death count is untrustworthy on the basis that the Gaza Health Ministry operates under Hamas governance.

"I have no notion that the Palestinians are telling the truth about how many people are killed," Biden told the press on Wednesday, adding, "I have no confidence in the number that the Palestinians are using."

Adam Taylor, the author of the aforementioned Washington Post article, correctly notes that Biden's statements are a bit odd given that his own State Department considered Gaza's Ministry of Health reliable enough to cite their death counts in its own reports as recently as a few months ago.

What changed? The information interests of the US empire changed.

When I drew attention to all this on Twitter a few hours ago I immediately started getting comments from Israel apologists dismissing the information I was providing because Human Rights Watch is bad and

Adam Taylor X
@mradamtaylor · Follow

Despite Biden's skepticism about Gaza Health Ministry death toll numbers, the State Department was citing them just a few months ago: state.gov/reports/2022-c...

Jeff Stein @JStein_WaPo
From @mradamtaylor on the Gaza Health Ministry's estimates of Palestinian death tolls:

washingtonpost.com/world/2023/10/...

Many experts consider figures provided by the ministry reliable, given its access, sources and accuracy in past statements.

Share this article

"Everyone uses the figures from the Gaza Health Ministry because those are generally proven to be reliable," said Omar Shakir, Israel and Palestine director at Human Rights Watch. "In the times in which we have done our own verification of numbers for particular strikes, I'm not aware of any time which there's been some major discrepancy."

Shakir said Human Rights Watch would not use figures provided by parties with "a propensity to misrepresent information."

"We know that a health ministry is going to base [death tolls] on assessments coming from hospitals, morgues, etc.," he said. "They have an ability to collect that in a way that other sources not there can't do."

6:26 AM · Oct 26, 2023

473 Reply Copy link

Read 25 replies

unreliable and because The Washington Post is bad and unreliable, in order to defend their belief that the Gaza Ministry of Health is bad and unreliable.

These are the tactics of people who have lost the argument. They understand that the soaring death counts from Israel's ongoing massacre of Palestinians in Gaza is devastating to the information interests of the side they support, so they need to make up fairy tales about how The Washington Post, Human Rights Watch and the US State Department have been engaged in a years-long conspiracy to make Israel look bad.

Which is of course not to say that anyone should ever believe claims made by The Washington Post or Human Rights Watch on blind faith—I've had major criticisms of both of these institutions myself over the years. Believing they're infallible would be as misguided as believing they're always lying.

Which is exactly the point I'm trying to make here: it's not about the source, it's about the strength of the argument. Attacking the source instead of attacking the argument is what people do when they can't attack the argument. It's a standard ad hominem.

A lot of people think an ad hominem is when you say something that hurts the feelings of somebody you disagree with, but that's not what that term refers to. An ad hominem is when you attack the character or motives of the person making the argument instead of attacking the argument itself; it's a fallacious debate tactic designed to move the conversation away from the pursuit of truth and facts to just dismissing someone's claims because you don't like them. It can be entirely appropriate to interrogate someone's motives and character when that's

the only information you've got to work with and is relevant to the conversation, but when it's used as a substitute for addressing evidence and argumentation it's a fallacy.

And that's the only tool Israel apologists seem to have in their toolbox these days. It's exactly what they are doing when they accuse you of being a "terrorist supporter" or an "anti-semite" when you criticize Israel; they cannot address your actual criticisms because Israel's actions in Gaza are indefensible, so they attempt to malign your character or your motives to shut down the debate and keep people from listening to you.

The "you can't trust those death counts because they come from the health ministry of an enemy government" line can be used in literally any war against literally any enemy. People who care about facts don't look at what governmental loyalties a source has, they look at whether the institutions in question have a track record of being reliable or not, and whether its claims are supported by evidence.

You'd have to be a complete idiot to look at the photos and videos showing entire city blocks reduced to rubble in an area known to be packed full of children and not assume that there is a massive number of civilian deaths in Gaza right now. As Antiwar's Dave DeCamp recently noted, dramatic increases in death counts in Gaza correspond directly with Israeli government statements about having increased the number of bombs dropped. This is what you would expect to see if the ministry was accurately reporting deaths.

Israel apologists are doing everything they can to minimize and justify Israel's crimes in every way possible, because if westerners start looking objectively at the crimes themselves they will cease consenting to this horrific genocidal massacre that western governments are fully supporting.

They don't have truth on their side, and they don't have morality on their side, so all they can ever do is attack the sources of the ideas and information that are opening people's eyes to the criminality of Israel and its western allies.

Featured image via Adobe Stock.

Bombing Kids And Blaming It On Hamas

The "human shields" narrative is just Israel bombing civilians and blaming it on someone else. That's all it's ever been.

The "human shields" argument is like if London had responded to an IRA attack by dropping thousands of bombs on Belfast, killing thousands of Irish civilians and hundreds of children, and justifying its bombing campaign by calling it an unfortunate but necessary measure to take out the IRA's Belfast Brigade because they're located in the same places as civilians.

It's like if the western political/media class defended and supported the carpet bombing of Belfast, saying "All those thousands of deaths are the fault of the IRA, because they're in Belfast where the civilians are. England has a right to defend itself, after all."

It's like if Belfast was walled in with nowhere for civilians to escape to, and London carpet bombed it targeting schools, churches and hospitals, and the western press framed this relentless assault on civilian buildings as "the UK-IRA war" in which London is exclusively bombing "IRA targets in Belfast".

It's like if the British spent a week dropping military explosives on locations it knew were packed with Irish children, and anyone who criticized this was accused of anti-Britishism and blood libel.

And to be clear this is not something I'd put past the British actually doing during the Troubles... if the Irish were Muslim and their skin was a little darker.

Featured image via Adobe Stock.

White House Says Continued Civilian Slaughter "Is Going To Happen" In Gaza

White House National Security Council spokesman John Kirby told the press that the continued killing of civilians in Israel's bombing campaign in Gaza "is going to happen".

"This is war," said Kirby. "It is combat. It is bloody, ugly and it's going to be messy, and innocent civilians are going to be hurt going forward. I wish I could tell you something different—I wish that wasn't gonna happen, but it is going to happen."

"And that doesn't make it right," Kirby added. "It doesn't make it dismissible. It doesn't mean that we aren't going to express concerns about that and do everything we can to help the Israelis do everything they can to minimize it. But that's unfortunately the nature of conflict."

Oh okay well as long as you're going to "express concerns".

The information interests of Israel and its western allies have been greatly served by framing this onslaught as a "war", when that label doesn't actually apply here. A war is when two nations or groups are in a state of armed combat with each other; one side may be more powerful than the other, but the combat is decidedly going two ways.

That's not what's happening here. Israel is raining high-tech military explosives upon civilian infrastructure inside a giant concentration camp densely populated with children, and every now and then a militant in Gaza fires back a type of rocket that is essentially a glorified firework which historically hardly ever kills anyone. Israel is killing civilians by the thousands and turning entire city blocks to rubble, while Hamas and other resistance groups in Gaza are doing some light property damage in what amounts to a performative display of defiance.

That's not a war. That's a massacre.

By calling this something that it isn't instead of what it is, Israel apologists are able to respond to all criticisms of its actions with a shrug and a "This is war, man. War is ugly, what can I tell ya?" They wouldn't be able to do that if they were addressing this atrocity truthfully.

The only thing truthful about Kirby's framing was his statement that the slaughter of civilians is going to keep happening. The death toll from airstrikes in Gaza has reportedly surpassed 6,500, with the 24-hour periods from Monday to Tuesday and Tuesday to Wednesday both exceeding 700 deaths each. As Antiwar's Dave DeCamp notes, this large escalation in deaths coincides with claims from Benjamin Netanyahu that Israel has escalated its bombing campaign.

This is all being funded and supported by the United States, who has been ramping up its military presence in the middle east in some pretty

disconcerting ways. Not one but two US aircraft carrier strike groups have been deployed to the eastern Mediterranean since the killing began, and the Pentagon has told the press that it expects a "significant escalation" in attacks on US troops in the middle east in response to Israel's relentless assault on Palestinian lives. US military advisers have been sent to Israel to help the IDF prepare for its ground invasion of Gaza, and as usual Australia is joining in the US warmongering by sending more troops to the middle east as well.

So we can expect a lot more killing in the near future, one way or the other. No meaningful pressure is being placed on Israel to stop butchering civilians, and an escalation into a broader war in the middle east is not at all outside the realm of possibility. Things could be headed in a direction that makes a genocidal massacre look like sunny days in retrospect.

·

US Warmongers Keep Pushing The Narrative That Hamas Is To Blame For All Deaths In Gaza

One thing I've been meaning to highlight for the last few days is the way US warmongers have been forcefully pushing the propaganda narrative that Hamas bears 100 percent responsibility for all deaths in Gaza, and Israel bears zero percent, as Israel ramps up its mass slaughter of Palestinians.

In a New York Times article titled "Hamas Bears the Blame for Every Death in This War," notorious neoconservative war propagandist Bret Stephens argues that no blame whatsoever should be placed on Israel for the thousands of civilians it has killed in its latest Gaza operation and the thousands more it will continue to kill.

"The central cause of Gaza's misery is Hamas," Stephens writes. "It alone bears the blame for the suffering it has inflicted on Israel and knowingly invited against Palestinians. The best way to end the misery is to remove the cause, not stay the hand of the remover."

Lindsey Graham (who is such a bloodthirsty psychopath that he recently called on Israel to "level" Gaza because "we're in a religious war here" and said the US should bomb Iran any time Hamas executes any prisoners) echoed Bret Stephens' sentiments during an interview on Monday.

"Every death going forward I blame on Hamas, not Israel," Graham said.

Graham's senatorial colleague Mitt Romney was even more direct.

"You are going to see pictures of Palestinian civilians that are going to be injured, killed by virtue of the conflict, which is ongoing," Romney said during an appearance in Tel Aviv. "I hope you recognize that those individuals are being killed because of Hamas, not because of Israel."

"They are using Palestinians to protect Hamas lives," Romney added. "Therefore, when Israel takes action to try and go after Hamas and take out its leadership, there will be civilians and innocents that will be killed. They will parade that

as if this is some horror perpetrated by Israel."

"Do not forget the lives that you will see lost on TV… Israeli lives and Palestinian lives [lost] are all the result of Hamas," Romney continued.

Fox News war slut Sean Hannity shares the same opinion, surprise surprise.

"Every single death in this conflict can be blamed on Hamas and their supporters in Iran," Hannity told his audience. "Because of last week's brutal terror attack, Israel has no choice. They must defend their country."

This is about as blatant as war propaganda gets. These imperial narrative managers are using their massive platforms and influence to tell everyone "Remember kids, you're going to see a whole bunch of innocent civilians get killed, and it's going to look a lot like those civilians are being killed by Israel. But don't you believe your lying eyes! They're really being killed by Hamas. Just because the people dropping military explosives in areas known to be packed full of children are wearing Israeli badges and operating Israeli war machinery doesn't mean Israel is involved in this butchery in any way. It's really Hamas doing all that."

And what's great about this narrative is that there's no upper limit on the extent to which it can be applied. If they wind up killing twenty thousand Gazans, then Hamas killed twenty

thousand Gazans. If they wind up killing a hundred thousand Gazans, then Hamas killed a hundred thousand Gazans. If they wind up driving all Palestinians out of Gaza into refugee camps in the Sinai desert and seizing that territory as their own, then god damn you for ethnic cleansing the Gaza Strip, Hamas.

No matter how far they extend the bloodshed and abuse, they can still blame it all on Hamas. Per this logic there is therefore no limit on how far things can be taken before the cost of human life and suffering outweighs Israel's strategic objectives and ceasefire negotiations become necessary. It's a catch-all innoculation against peace.

And to be honest it seems to be working; I get a constant barrage of "Hamas is to blame for this" comments on social media whenever talking about Israel's obvious criminality in this current crisis.

This propaganda is being pushed as President Biden vows to support Israel's ongoing Gaza massacre and tells Netanyahu the US is fully behind Israel's planned Gaza ground invasion.

Not only is Israel absolutely responsible for the bloodshed it chooses to inflict on the people of Gaza, the United States is too. These crimes are being perpetrated with US weapons, US funding and US consent, and backed by the full might of the US propaganda machine. The US is just as responsible for the destruction of Gaza as Israel is.

All this propaganda is designed to keep people from assigning any blame or responsibility to those who are most guilty in this onslaught, because if everyone clearly understood what's being done in their name, all that carefully manufactured consent would rapidly disintegrate.

Featured image via Gage Skidmore (CC BY-SA 2.0 Deed)

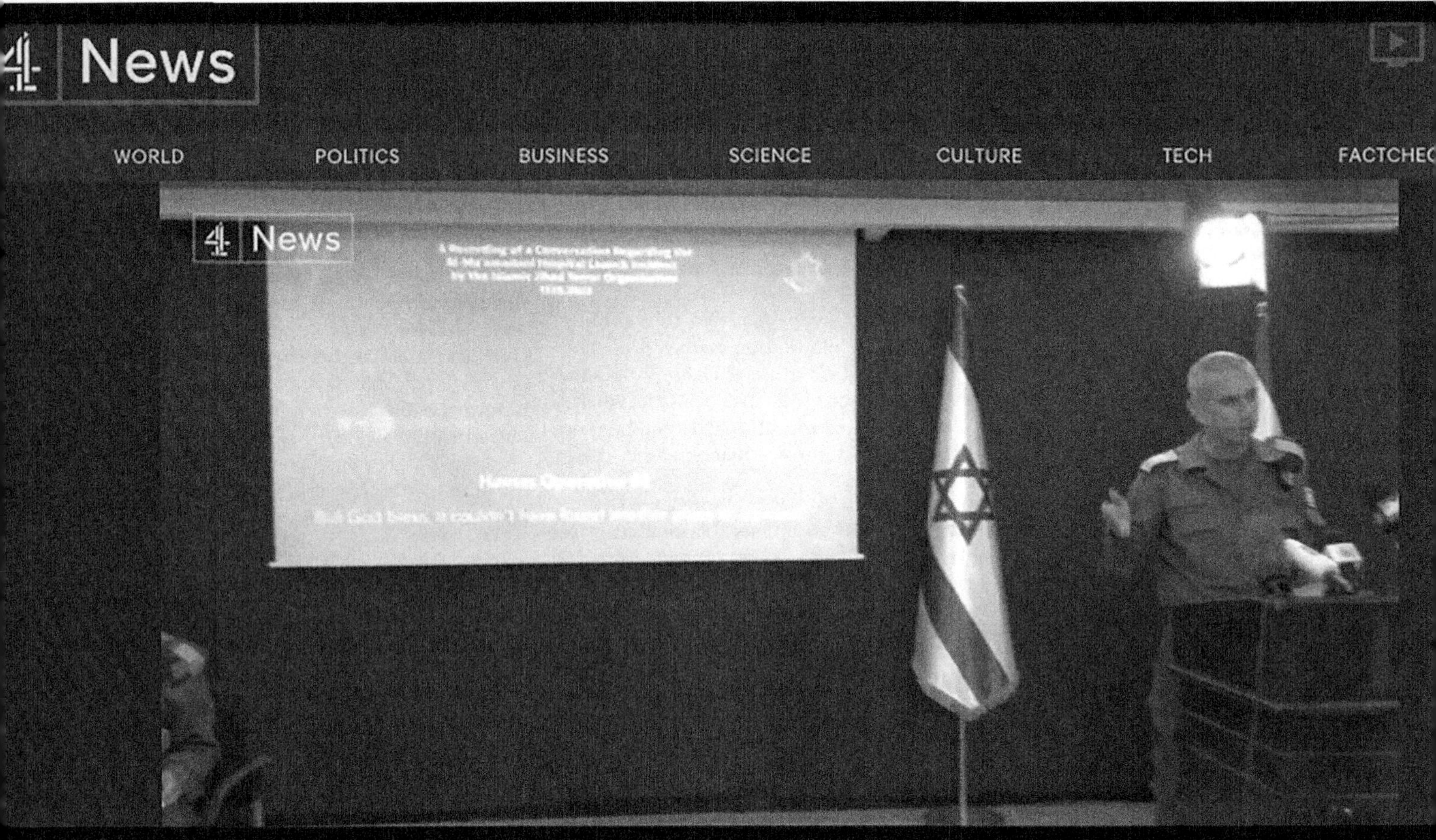

The Mainstream Press Keep Slamming Israel's Hospital Bombing Story

A new report from the UK's Channel 4 News adds to the surprising amount of opposition we're seeing in the mainstream press to Israel's narrative about the deadly explosion at the Al-Ahli Arab Hospital in Gaza this past Tuesday.

The report, led by Channel 4 chief correspondent Alex Thomson, spotlights glaring plot holes in Israel's claim that a failed rocket by Palestinian Islamic Jihad was responsible for the blast, and in the supposed audio clip Israel published which it claims is an intercepted conversation between two Hamas fighters saying Israel was not responsible. It also presents an argument that will be inconvenient for Israel apologists who've been claiming photos of the damage to the hospital rule out the possibility of an Israeli airstrike.

"So what of Israel's explanation?" says Thomson. "Sensing a major problem they worked through the night to get their version out. Press conference first thing. Conclusion: an Islamic Jihad rocked caused it all."

"They present what they say is two Hamas operatives talking about the attack," Thomson reports. "Hamas call this an obvious fabrication. Two independent Arab journalists told us the same thing, because of the language, accent, dialect, syntax and tone. None of which is, they say, credible."

"Equally, Israel claims the Islamic Jihad failed missile was fired from here: a cemetery very close to the hospital," Thomson continues.

"But look again at the video of the event—the trajectory of the missile doesn't line up with that location. Too high. Too horizontal. Confusingly, the Israelis' presentation also says the missile was fired from a location down in the southwest; it can't be both."

Thomson also reports that while the photos of the blast site do appear to rule out a ground-detonating Israeli munition, they're entirely in keeping with other munitions used by Israel which could easily have taken such a toll on human life.

"This is what you see at the hospital today—small craters you'd expect to see from a mortar strike or artillery round, not a missile," says Thomson. "Surrounding buildings have only superficial damage, not structural collapse. Some of the windows of an

alex thomson
@alextomo · Follow
The explosive site at the hospital in no way matches that of a ground- burst Israeli missile strike . But that doesn't discount drone or other airburst munitions used by Israel.
2:48 AM · Oct 19, 2023
497   Reply   Copy link
Read 51 replies

adjoining church remain intact. This makes a ground-detonating Israeli missile strike unlikely, but it doesn't rule out an airburst munition, which could cause major loss of life, but would produce far less structural damage."

Thomson also notes that "Israel has form when it comes to war propaganda", citing its false denials of the IDF killings of British filmmaker James Miller and Palestinian-American journalist Shireen Abu Akleh.

On Twitter (or whatever we're calling it now), Thomson's remarks on the Israeli audio file were even more pointed.

"Several experts confirm Hamas' view to Channel 4 News that the audio tape of 'Hamas' operatives talking about the missile malfunction is a fake," tweeted Thomson. "They say the tone, syntax, accent and idiom are absurd."

This is a still developing story with much still to be revealed, but this to me might be the most damning evidence against Israel yet. If Israel didn't bomb that hospital, then why is it publishing fake audio clips of people posing as Hamas fighters agreeing with each other that Israel definitely didn't bomb that hospital?

I mean, if people were saying I bombed a hospital, and I knew I didn't, the last thing I'd do is publish an audio file of me pretending to be two guys talking about how Caitlin definitely didn't bomb the hospital.

Picture a recording of me doing two blokey-sounding voices going,

"Hello my evil friend!"

"Hello!"

"Did you hear that Caitlin definitely did not bomb that hospital?"

"She didn't?"

"No! It turns out it was we, the Evil Bad Guys!"

"We did it?"

"Yes, it was us!"

That would look pretty silly, right?

If Israel is making itself look this ridiculous, then it's no wonder the western press are not lining up to help it cover up this particular misdeed. They've got to maintain at least some credibility if they're going to keep manufacturing consent for other wars, after all.

·

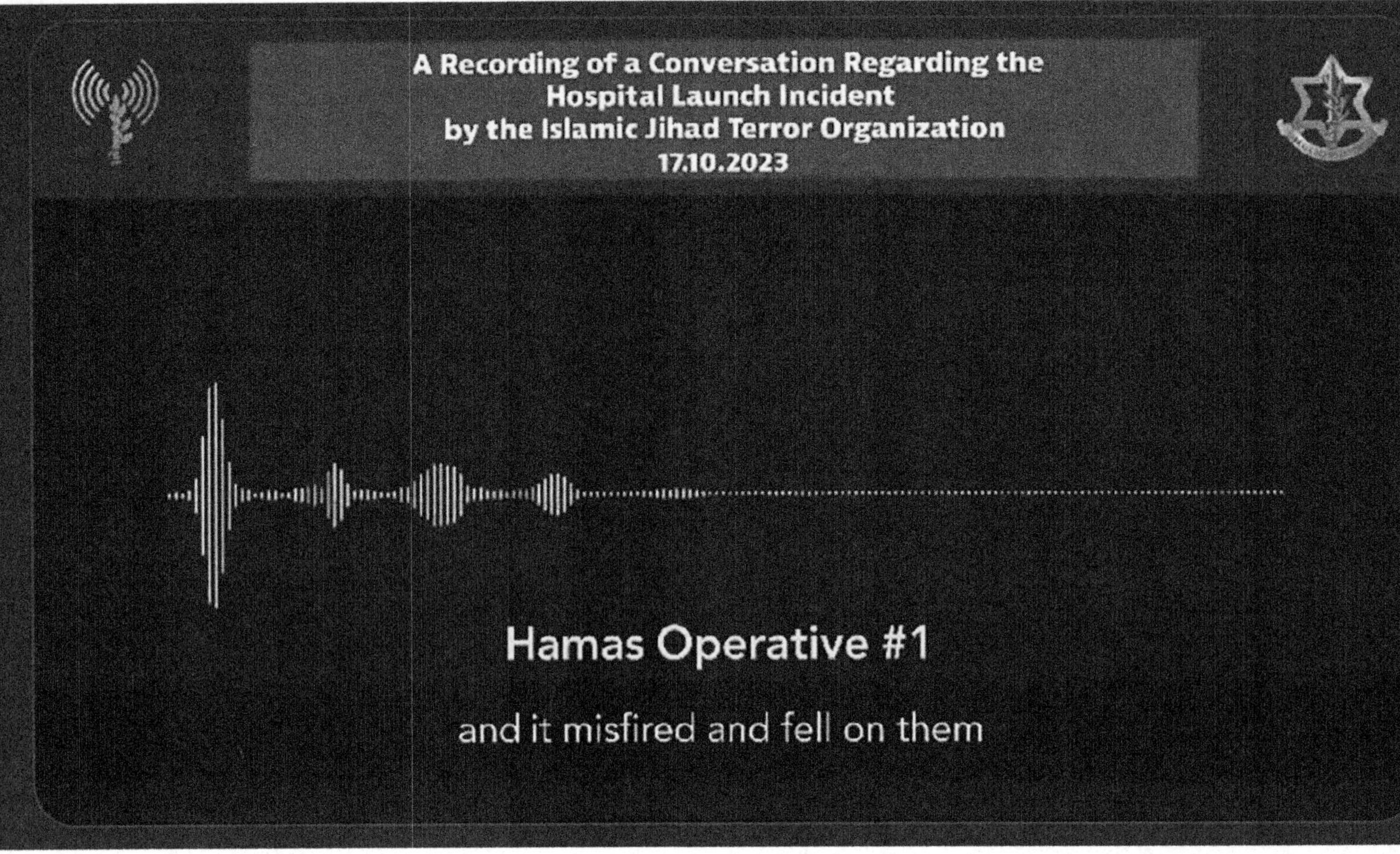

Israeli Intelligence Suddenly Able To Intercept Hamas Communications

Another strange thing about Israel's claim that its intelligence services didn't detect preparations for the Hamas attack on October 7 is the fact that it is now releasing what it claims are intercepted conversations of Hamas fighters talking to each other about matters of high importance.

Israel has released an audio clip of two voices which it claims belong to Hamas militants speaking about the hotly disputed explosion at the Al-Ahli Arab Hospital in Gaza on Tuesday. The IDF had previously told the press that it would be releasing intercepted conversations which prove Palestinian Islamic Jihad, not Israel, was responsible for the blast.

Here's a transcript of Israel's English translation of the dialogue:

Hamas Operative #2: I'm telling you this is the first time that we see a missile like this failing and so that's why we are saying it belongs to the Palestinian Islamic Jihad.

Hamas Operative #1: What?

Hamas Operative #2: They are saying it belongs to Palestinian Islamic Jihad

Hamas Operative #1: It's from us?

#2: It looks like it

#1: Who says this?

#2: They are saying that the shrapnel from the missile is local shrapnel and not like Israeli shrapnel

#1: What are you saying (name bleeped)?

#2: But God bless, it couldn't have found another place to explode?

#1: Nevermind, (name bleeped), yes they shot it from the cemetery behind the hospital

#2: What?

#1: They shot it coming from the cemetery behind the Al-Ma'amadani Hospital, and it misfired and fell on them

#2: There is a cemetery behind it?

#1: Yes, Al-Ma'amadani is exactly in the compound

#2: Where is it when you enter the compound?

#1: You first enter the compound and don't go towards the city and it's on the right side of the Al-Ma'amadani Hospital.

#2: Yes , I know it.

You can make of this transcript what you wish. I've seen plenty of people on the pro-Palestinian side of the debate disputing the veracity of the recording for a variety of reasons, from claiming Gazans don't speak in the accent used in the clip to claiming Hamas fighters don't communicate such information over the phone or without using codes for locations. But I personally am completely unqualified to make such assessments, so I'll leave that question alone for the time being.

All I'd like to highlight at the moment is the fact that it sure is interesting how Israel suddenly claims to have

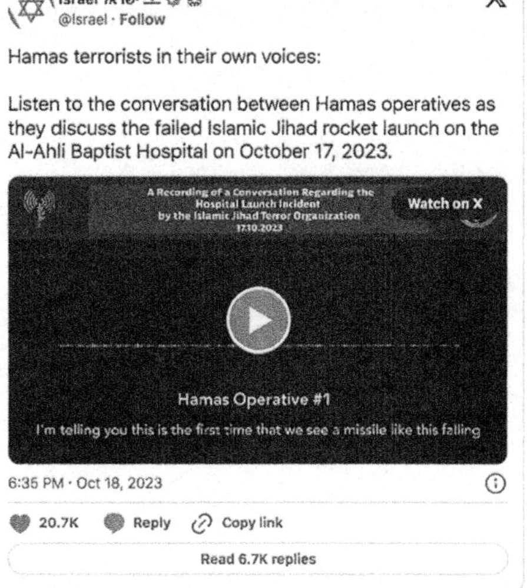

all this visibility into conversations between Hamas fighters about combat operations against Israel. Where was all this eavesdropping capability while Hamas was preparing a massive assault that wound up killing over a thousand people?

It's certainly possible that Israeli intelligence services are phenomenal at spying on Hamas communications, and it's certainly possible that Israeli intelligence services had no idea Hamas was preparing its attack. It's also possible that both are false. But it's very difficult to believe they're both true.

It's very hard to believe that Israel had all this insight into what Hamas fighters are communicating about but somehow missed preparations for a highly sophisticated multi-pronged attack involving motorboats, drones and motorized paragliders in an area the size of Philadelphia. It's even harder to believe it when you learn that Egyptian intelligence warned Israel of a coming attack shortly before it happened. It's harder still when you learn that according to CNN, US officials were circulating "reporting from Israel indicating unusual activity by Hamas" on October 6. Even harder when you learn that Hamas itself was reportedly greatly surprised by how many Israelis they were able to kill and how many hostages they were able to take.

One of the many problems with the bizarre mainstream consensus that it's fine for nations to go on a murderous rampage whenever something bad happens to them—as we saw from the US after 9/11 and are seeing again in Israel—is that it gives sociopathic intelligence agencies an obvious and undeniable incentive to let bad things happen in order to advance pre-existing agendas that can only be advanced by mass-scale military violence. Whether that's happening in this particular case or not, it would be wise to remove this incentive by insisting on cool heads and rational responses to attacks when they occur.

•

Mass Media Reporters Aren't Buying Israel's Hospital Bombing Story

A huge blast in Gaza has occurred at the Al-Ahli Arab Hospital, reportedly killing hundreds of people. The exact death toll is still unknown.

Details of who is responsible for the explosion are being hotly debated by all parties, and this is still a developing story with a lot of details yet to be revealed. But what I'd like to quickly document as things unfold is the highly unusual number of mass media reporters I've been seeing who haven't hesitated to point to Israel as the probable culprit.

After noting that Israel is blaming the blast on a failed rocket launch by Palestinian Islamic Jihad (PIJ), MSNBC foreign correspondent Raf Sanchez quickly pointed out that PIJ rockets don't tend to do that kind of damage, but Israeli missiles do. He also noted that Israel has an extensive history of lying about this sort of thing.

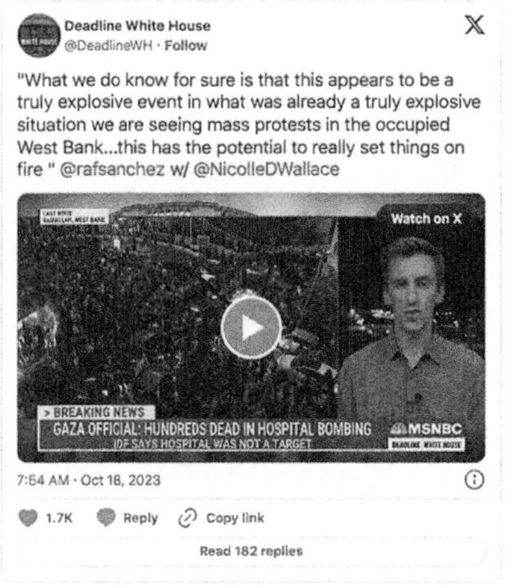

"The Israeli military at this point is not providing any evidence to back up its claims that this was a Palestinian Islamic Jihad rocket; they are citing intelligence that they have not yet made public," Sanchez said. "We should also say that this kind of death toll is not what you normally associate with Palestinian rockets. These rockets are dangerous, they are deadly, they do not tend to kill hundreds of people in a single strike in the way that Israeli high explosives—especially these bunker buster bombs that are used to target these Hamas tunnels under Gaza City—do have the potential to kill hundreds of people."

"And we should say finally that there are instances in the past where the Israeli military has said things in the immediate aftermath of an incident that have turned out not to be true in the long run," Sanchez added. "And the one example I'll give you is that when the Al Jazeera journalist, Shireen Abu Akleh, was killed in the occupied West Bank, the Israeli military initially said that she was killed by Palestinian gunmen, and it was only months and months later that they admitted that it was likely an Israeli soldier who fired the fatal shot."

CNN's Clarissa Ward said essentially the same thing.

"I will say, just based on seeing these rocket attacks many times over the years, that they don't usually have an impact like that in terms of the size of the blast, in terms of the scale of the death toll and the scale of the damage," Ward said. "It's also not the first time, it's important to add, that we have seen the IDF categorically deny something before being forced to kind of do an about-face after an extensive investigation."

BBC foreign correspondent Jon Donnison gave basically the same opinion.

"It's hard to see what else this could be, really, given the size of the explosion, other than an Israeli air strike, or several air strikes," Donnison said from Jerusalem. "Because, you know, when we've seen rockets being fired out of Gaza, we never see explosions of that scale. We might see half a dozen, maybe a few more people being killed in such rocket attacks, but we've never seen anything on the scale of the sort of explosion on the video I was watching earlier."

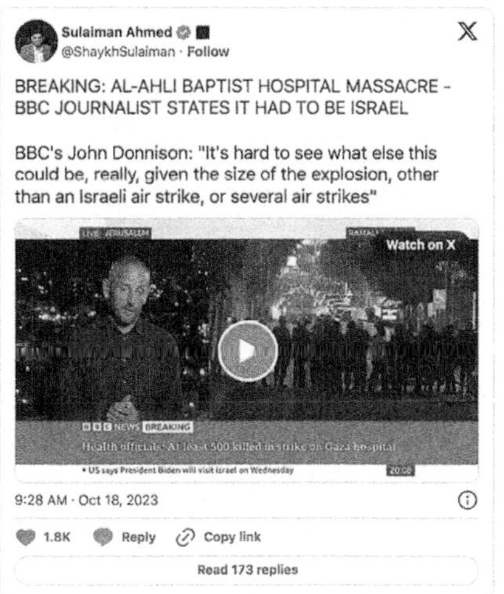

That's three mass media reporters that I've seen just in my random information-gathering meanderings—not on their personal social media accounts, but live on air.

It's highly unusual to see this degree of skepticism in the western

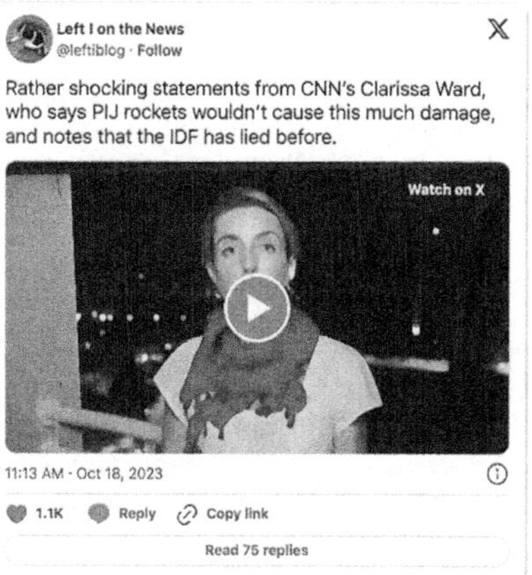

press right off the bat when it goes against the information interests of Israel specifically or the US power alliance more generally. Typically we've been seeing the media uncritically report unverified claims about Palestinian militants while expressing rigorous skepticism solely toward any information which might benefit the Palestinian resistance, so there's clearly something about this particular story which makes mass media reporters remarkably reluctant to push the Israeli narrative.

Maybe they're getting information in their group chats which has caused them to keep Israel's claims about the hospital bombing at arm's length, or maybe they're just looking at the facts and deciding this narrative is too flimsy to get behind. If it looks like Israel's version of events will fall apart after investigation, they're not going to want to stake their reputation and their pride on pushing it with their usual gusto during an Israeli military operation that is facing unusually intense scrutiny from the entire world.

Israel does after all have an extensive history of attacking hospitals and healthcare facilities, including in this current operation in Gaza, including apparently bombing this exact same hospital just a few days ago. ReliefWeb, which is run by the United Nations Office for the Coordination of Humanitarian Affairs, recently published a report on the numerous Israeli strikes that have hit hospitals, ambulances and healthcare workers between October 12 and October 15, and listed among the hospitals hit is the Ahli Arab Hospital in Gaza City—the same hospital that was just destroyed a few days later.

Citing "Al Jazeera V and Personal Communication," ReliefWeb reports the following:

"14 October 2023: In Gaza city city and governorate, Ahli Arab Hospital was hit by Israeli airstrikes, partially damaging two floors and damaging the ultrasound and mammography room. Four people were injured."

It's also probably worth noting that according to the World Health Organization this hospital was one of the twenty hospitals which the IDF had ordered to evacuate because of the aggressions it was planning to inflict on that part of Gaza.

Again, information is still coming in and this developing story could possibly wind up looking very different from what it looks like right now. But if I was an Israel apologist, I don't think I'd find the current winds in the mass media very encouraging.

UPDATE: A previous version of this article referred to the hospital as having been "destroyed". Subsequently revealed photographic evidence shows the hospital still standing, with some analysis suggesting that this probably rules out a ground-burst Israeli airstrike, but not a strike by drone or other airburst munitions used by Israel.

.

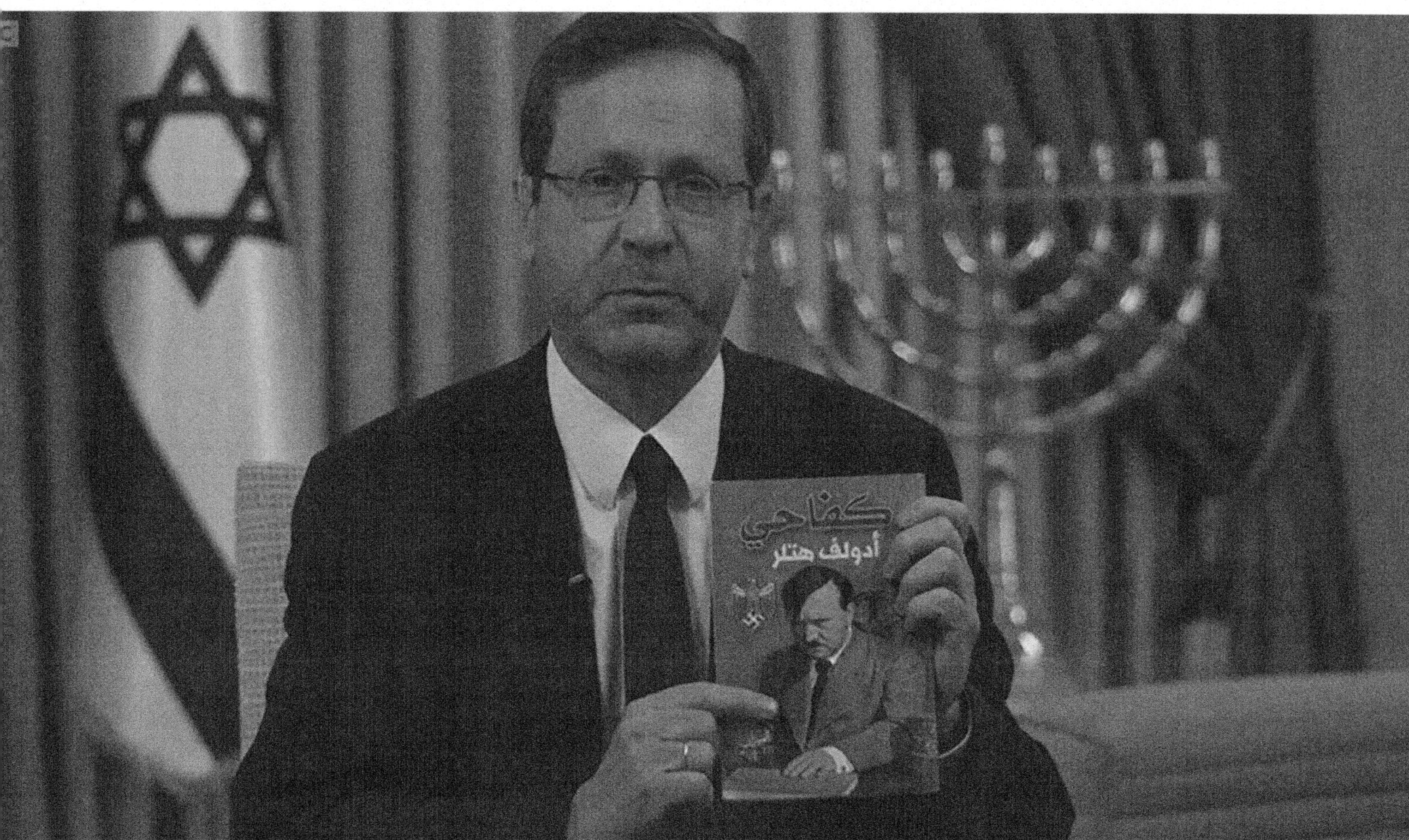

They're Just Insulting Our Intelligence At This Point
More Notes From The Edge Of The Narrative Matrix

Americans: healthcare please

US government: Sorry did you say billions of dollars for ethnic cleansing in the middle east?

Americans: no, healthcare

US government. Alright, you drive a hard bargain but here's billions of dollars for ethnic cleansing in the middle east.

.

Here's a tip: the side that keeps having to come up with justifications and explanations for why it's fine and normal for them to be killing thousands of children and perpetrating ethnic cleansing is probably not the side that's in the right.

.

I used to think it was bad for Israel to be massacring children by the thousands and bombing hospitals and shooting quadriplegics and children in hospital beds, but then Israel's president waved an Arabic translation of Mein Kampf in front of a camera so now I think it's good.

.

If Israel's position were based on truth and morality it wouldn't be churning out a nonstop deluge of obvious lies.

No one believes anything Israel says anymore. You either know Israel lies constantly or you know it but pretend you don't.

.

You know how narcissists will do the most fucked up shit and if anyone calls them out they act all wounded and victimized like "Oh, what, I'm the bad guy now??" That's Israel and its supporters.

.

Anyone who criticizes US-sponsored military violence gets accused of supporting the other side by supporters of that military violence. If you opposed the Iraq invasion you were a Saddam supporter, if you criticized US proxy warfare in Ukraine you were a Putin lover, etc. The argument is that criticizing the actions of the world's most powerful war machine means you support the side opposing that war machine, and because you're a treasonous monster who supports the other side that means your

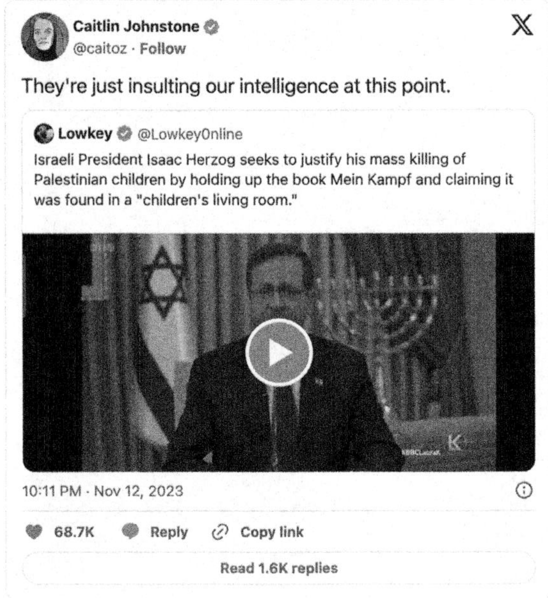

criticisms should not be listened to.

This happens with literally every single high-profile act of US interventionism. Literally every single one, without a single, solitary exception. What this means in effect is that all criticism of the world's most powerful war machine is considered unacceptable and gets stomped down. Those who are calling you a Hamas lover and a terrorist sympathizer today are telling you that nobody should ever criticize any US-sponsored act of military aggression, because they're using the exact same tactic that is literally always used to stomp out all US-sponsored acts of military aggression.

What they are really saying when they call you a Hamas supporter is, "Shut up. Be silent. Never criticize US warmongering. Never criticize the most consequential actions of the most powerful and destructive government on this planet, under any circumstances. Shut up. Be silent. Obey."

.

It's not okay for grown adults to believe Israel is "liberating" the people of Gaza.

.

The correct response to learning that Hamas has significant support in Gaza is not "Oh well exterminate everyone in Gaza then," it's "Wow, how hellish must Israel have made life in Gaza for that to be the case?"

.

It's true that a Republican president would be as bad as Biden on Israel-Palestine, but the correct response to that isn't "Oh well I'll vote Democrat then," it's "If we're not allowed to vote on whether our government murders children that means the entire system needs to go."

.

What's wild is that this right now is the best the west will ever look regarding this Gaza issue. Public approval of a depraved western military action is always highest at the beginning, then as time goes on people start to realize they were lied to, and information starts coming out proving the whole thing was a sham. We've seen it over and over and over again, from Vietnam to Iraq to Afghanistan to Libya. Already people are starting to realize the proxy war in Ukraine was a terrible idea, and in a few years no serious person will dispute this.

But this time the western-backed destruction of Gaza is facing massive public disapproval when it's just over a month old. As more and more information comes out and more and more westerners become aware of what exactly their governments supported in Gaza, it's going to get much, much worse. That's why you're seeing billionaires freaking out and getting together to set up narrative management operations to try and manipulate public perception; they know they're losing control of the narrative, and losing it much, much earlier than they should be.

But there's only so many ways you can spin the murder of thousands of children. The old propaganda methods just aren't working the way they usually do. Eyes are starting to open. People are starting to get angry. And the powers that rule over us are starting to get very, very nervous.

.

Caitlin Johnstone ✓
@caitoz · **Follow**

There is nothing more liberal than conducting a genocide in the middle east while waving pride flags as Hollywood goons applaud your brave progressivism.

leekern ✓ @leekern13

LIBERATION▬THE FIRST EVER PRIDE FLAG RAISED IN GAZA!

Under Hamas, being gay means death. Israeli Yoav Atzmoni wanted to send a message of hope. See his story below.

To Gaza's hidden LGBTQ+ community: STAY HOPEFUL of a future where you can live and love free of Hamas!

10:04 AM · Nov 13, 2023

❤ **2.6K**   💬 **Reply**   🔗 **Copy link**

Read 62 replies

The World Is Being Blinded To What's Happening In Gaza

Great efforts are being made to hide what's happening in Gaza from the outside world, both by Israel and its western allies.

Israel's minister of communications announced on Friday that all internet services in Gaza would be cut off on Saturday; CNN reports that internet services there have already been plummeting for the last week. Electronic Intifada director Ali Abunimah recently said on Twitter that he hasn't been able to reach any of his contacts in Gaza for hours.

Even before the internet was cut off it had already been getting harder and harder for people in Gaza to get information to the outside world after Israel cut the enclave off from electricity as part of its "complete siege" on the civilian population. The outlet Middle East Eye reports that it lost contact with two of its journalists in Gaza on Friday. One of them, a reporter named Maha Hussaini, posted a video before losing contact in which she said "This might be my last video, as my phone battery is dying while we're facing an almost complete blackout."

As usual, Israel has also been targeting members of the press. A Reuters journalist was killed and six others from Reuters, AFP and Al Jazeera were injured by IDF artillery fire in southern Lebanon on Friday. Outlets like The New York Times and even Reuters have refrained from acknowledging the perpetrator of the attack, but Al Jazeera attributes the casualties to "shelling by Israeli forces," citing witness testimony. BBC journalists were also held at gunpoint and physically assaulted by Israeli soldiers in Tel Aviv, and it's probably worth mentioning that these reporters were specifically from BBC Arabic and had Arabic names.

Efforts to blind the world to Israel's crimes are of course not limited to Israel. The EU has begun exerting pressure on Twitter to begin censoring content on the Israel-Palestine issue in accordance with new Digital Services Act regulations in order to avoid receiving penalties. The day after receiving a 24-hour deadline to address "illegal content and disinformation," hundreds of "accounts linked to Hamas" were reportedly removed from the platform. We're meant to simply take it on faith that these accounts were indeed linked to Hamas and not simply deemed guilty of wrongthink.

Efforts to spread awareness of Israel's

crimes via public demonstrations have also been getting the blindfold treatment in the west. France has issued a blanket ban on all pro-Palestinian protests. Germany has been banning specific pro-Palestine protests and groups and has issued a total ban on all demonstrations deemed supportive of Hamas, and the Berlin public prosecutor's office has criminalized the use of the phrase "From the river to the sea, Palestine will be free."

In a new report for Mintpress News titled "Propaganda Blitz: How Mainstream Media is Pushing Fake Palestine Stories," Alan MacLeod documents how the western media have been further obfuscating pubic perception into what's happening in Gaza by pushing brazen atrocity propaganda and deceitfully framing the issue in a way that's wildly biased in favor of Israel's information interests.

So you can see that in every possible way, the world's vision into what's happening in Gaza is being obstructed, manipulated, and outright hidden. This is happening for the same reason witnesses to Mafia crimes tend to go missing: it's easier to get away with murder when there's nobody who saw you do it.

This is after all happening as Israel prepares to ramp up its aggressions even further, and as Israeli president Isaac Herzog asserts that there are no innocent civilians in Gaza because they didn't forcibly overthrow Hamas.

"It is an entire nation out there that is responsible," Herzog told the press on Friday. "It is not true this rhetoric about civilians not being aware, not involved. It's absolutely not true. They could have risen up. They could have fought against that evil regime which took over Gaza in a coup d'etat."

The worse Israel makes itself look with its own actions, the more forceful it and the nations who are aligned with it will get at obstructing and manipulating public perception of those actions. The more brazen Israel's criminality becomes, the more shrill and vitriolic its defenders will become, the more iron-fisted government interference in public opposition will get, and the more hidden what's happening in Gaza will become.

Internet blackouts, the war on

journalism, propaganda, influence operations, bans on demonstrations and online censorship are all happening for the same reason: to keep the public from forming a truth-based understanding of what's happening in Gaza. Because if the public did form a truth-based understanding of what's happening in Gaza, they wouldn't consent to what's happening there.

Featured image by Adobe Stock

Israel Is Just A Nonstop Bombing Campaign With A Flag
More Notes From The Edge Of The Narrative Matrix

It's not okay for grown adults to believe Hamas attacked Israel without provocation, solely because they are Bad Guys who are Bad. That kind of infantile fiction has no place outside of a children's cartoon show. You have access to a whole internet full of information. Use it.

.

It's cute how Israel apologists think accusing someone of being a terrorist supporter will work on anyone over 30. We saw this exact same schtick after 9/11, kids. The exact same vitriol, the exact same shrieking emotional hysteria. You were wrong then. You're wrong now.

.

Talking about the causes of attacks always gets you accused of supporting the attackers. Talking about the well-documented western provocations which led to the invasion of Ukraine gets you accused of loving Putin and being a Russian troll. Talking about the well-documented apartheid abuses which led to the Hamas attack gets you called a terrorist supporter, which is also exactly what happened after 9/11 if you talked about the well-documented provocations which led to the rise of Al Qaeda.

You're not allowed to talk about the actual reasons why bad things happened, you're only allowed to talk about the bad things and call them bad. If you ascribe any causation at all to the bad things which happened, the causation must solely and exclusively be that Bad Guys did them because the Bad Guys are Bad.

You are required to turn yourself into an unthinking mental infant who can only relate to world events by pointing at them and yelling "GOOD!" or "BAD!", with "good" and "bad" always perfectly aligning with the information interests of the US-centralized empire.

If the answers go against the information interests of the US-centralized empire, then you're not allowed to ask the questions. You can only believe what the talking heads tell you to believe and clap along to the beat of the imperial drum, like a child clapping along to a song on a cartoon show.

When empire simps berate you and accuse you of treasonous malfeasance for talking about the causes of terrible world events, what they are really saying is, "Stop asking questions. Stop thinking. Believe only what you are told. Become stupid. Become a drooling moron with American flags in your eyes. Stop using that tongue to question authority and affix it firmly to the imperial boot forever."

If you can't talk about the causes of violence, then you can't prevent violence. So if you're an empire that's held together by endless violence, that's the last thing you want people doing.

.

A guy stole my phone. Wasn't sure where he was staying so I had to set fire to the entire neighborhood. A lot of people died, but it's his fault for being where noncombatants are. He was using his neighbors as human shields. He is 100% responsible for their deaths, not me.

.

Electronic Intifada reports that an Israeli woman who was taken hostage at the rave on October 7 told Israeli media that she watched other hostages get mowed down by IDF troops who were firing indiscriminately on Hamas fighters.

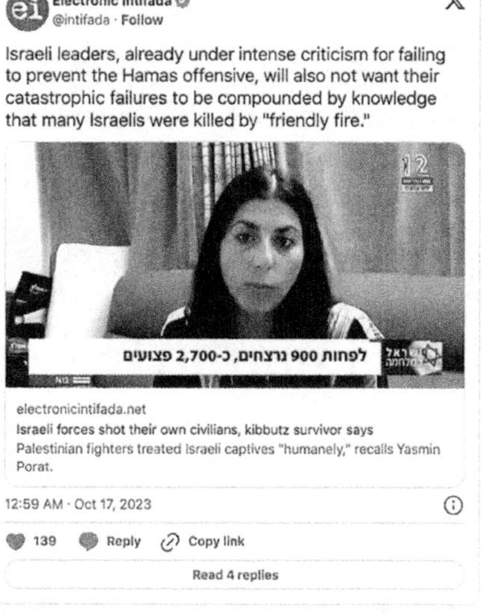

"They eliminated everyone, including the hostages," she told Israeli radio. "There was very, very heavy crossfire" and even tank shelling.

This will never, ever be acknowledged. If they're blaming Hamas for all Gazans killed by Israeli bombs, they're sure as hell going to blame Hamas for Israeli hostages killed by friendly fire.

.

Israeli rightists are so bat shit insane that they literally assaulted and spit on the families of the Israeli hostages for trying to keep their loved ones alive.

.

Normalize the phrase "the nonstop bombing campaign known as the nation of Israel".

.

I decided years ago never to get sucked into the dopey herd mentality demands to publicly "condemn" or "denounce" or "stand with" anyone whenever something bad happens. It's such a cringey example of the phony Instagram activism that has come to supplant real political engagement these days. If you have a position just use your brain and articulate yourself in your own words like a normal human being.

.

End the apartheid regime, establish equal rights for all, and all wealthy governments who've been backing Israel's abuses pay so many reparations to Palestinians that they can live a quality of life so high it will be like the abuse never occurred.

Featured image via Adobe Stock.

The US Is Just As Culpable As Israel For The Atrocities Committed In Gaza

The Israeli government dropped thousands of leaflets on Gaza telling everyone who lives in the northern part of the strip that they have 24 hours to evacuate to the southern part, and then bombed the people who were trying to evacuate.

United Nations spokesman Stephane Dujarric denounced the evacuation order, saying the UN "considers it impossible for such a movement to take place without devastating humanitarian consequences." Many Palestinians have said they're going to stay where they are because they have nowhere safe to go, despite being told by Israel they must leave if they want to "save their lives".

We're about to see the death and destruction get much, much worse in Gaza, and it's already very, very bad. As of this writing the official death toll from Israeli airstrikes in Gaza is speeding past 1,900, a number which includes 614 children. The primary job of Israel apologists in the coming days will be producing and circulating narratives explaining why this self-evidently terrible thing is actually perfectly fine and acceptable.

It's so incredibly obvious what we're looking at here. The only thing putting a wobble on people's perception is the immense amount of propaganda distortion the media is churning out on this issue, plus the fact that the demographics look a bit different from what history has conditioned people to watch out for. If there were two million Jewish people trapped by Christians in a giant concentration camp and placed under total siege, being told that half of them had 24 hours to relocate into the other half or be killed, nobody would have any confusion about what they were witnessing.

And top-down commands are being issued within the US government to support this massacre unconditionally.

The Huffington Post reports that the State Department has been circulating internal emails telling staff to avoid calls for peace, instructing them to refrain from using phrases like "de-escalation/ceasefire," "end to violence/bloodshed" and "restoring calm."

Asked about progressive congressional members calling for a ceasefire, White House press secretary Karine Jean-Pierre said, "we believe they are wrong, we believe they're repugnant, and we believe they're disgraceful."

On the question of whether there are any potential Israeli actions that the White House would not tolerate, US national security adviser Jake Sullivan told reporters "I'm not here

to draw red lines or issue warnings or give lectures to anybody."

So be perfectly clear, the US government is fully behind this massacre, and is just as culpable for everything that happens in Gaza as the Israeli government. These abuses are being perpetrated using US weapons, US funding and US consent. Washington could end this mass atrocity with a word, and instead they're fully aligning themselves behind it. Israel's crimes in Gaza are not meaningfully separate from the crimes of the US war machine.

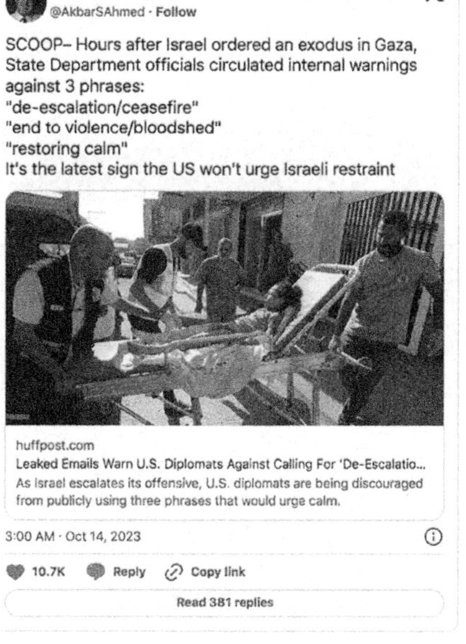

This is just a continuation and extension of the violence and bloodshed the US government has been inflicting around the world for generations. There's a clip of George W Bush going around from a California event on Tuesday in which, for some bizarre, unfathomable reason, the former president was asked to provide his opinion on what Israel should do in response to the Hamas attack on October 7.

Bush said pretty much what you'd expect him to say: "You're dealing with cold-blooded killers," "negotiating with killers is not an option," "one side is guilty." The same book he's been reciting from since

September 11, 2001. What I find much more interesting is, why is anyone asking the absolute worst person you could possibly ask about what should be done in response to such an attack?

I mean, Bush is literally the very last person in the entire world who anyone should be asking what to do in this situation. Literally dead last; there are eight billion people walking this earth right now who are infinitely more qualified to answer such questions than George W Bush. The agendas Bush set out to advance in the wake of 9/11 plunged the middle east into violence and chaos which wound up killing millions and displacing tens of millions, all supposedly in response to an attack which killed three thousand. What is this man doing holding a microphone and publicly opining on what Israel should do in response to the Hamas attack?

As we discussed earlier, 9/11 marked the beginning of some of the most deadly and catastrophic decisions ever made in US history. Israel has demonstrated that it is eager to repeat these profoundly depraved decisions to the furthest extent possible, and the US has demonstrated that it will fully support it in doing so.

The is because the United States never learned any moral lessons from its warmongering after 9/11—if it had, George W Bush would be sitting in a prison cell, and the US wouldn't be backing a mass atrocity in Gaza. The US-centralized empire is the most murderous and tyrannical power structure on earth, of which Israel's criminality is just one component.

Featured image via Adobe Stock.

Israeli Intelligence Suddenly Knows Exactly Where Hamas Is

It's interesting how on October 7 Israel had no idea what Hamas was up to, and yet from the beginning of the bombing campaign they know every mosque, school and hospital that Hamas is hiding in.

When you live under an empire of lies you'll be asked to believe a lot of very stupid things. The dumbest thing we're being asked to believe this week is that Israel's intelligence services are simultaneously so incompetent that Saturday's Hamas attack took them completely by surprise, but also so competent that all the buildings they're destroying with their relentless bombing campaign on Gaza are directed solely at Hamas.

The phrase "Hamas targets" has been all over the news media the last few days in reference to the ongoing attacks on Gaza, which have as of this writing killed over 1,500 Palestinians, a third of them children.

"Israel conducts large-scale strikes on Hamas targets," reads a CNN headline.

"Israel conducts 'large-scale strike' on Hamas targets," reads the title of

a segment for ABC News.

"Israel says it dropped 6,000 bombs so far against Hamas targets," reads a report by The Washington Post.

Gosh, Israel must have really great visibility into Gaza to know that each of those 6,000 bombs was aimed "Hamas targets" and not just civilian buildings.

Where was this 20/20 vision when Hamas was preparing for an attack using motorized paragliders, drones and motorboats in an enclosed strip of land the size of Philadelphia? How did Israeli intelligence fail to detect preparations for this attack even after Egyptian intelligence warned them that it was coming? How did they fail so spectacularly that even Hamas was reportedly surprised by the scale of their operation's success? Is it really reasonable to believe they were blind as moles to Hamas activity last week but have the eye of the eagle this week?

President Biden made some noises on Wednesday about how important it is that Israel "operate by the rules of war", which sounded like empty cover-your-ass narrative fluff even before we heard US National Security Advisor Jake Sullivan dismiss any notion of "red lines" that Israel must not cross in Gaza.

Not even mainstream empire apologists are buying it. Politico's Andrew Ward, in an article sponsored by Lockheed Martin in which he writes that "Israel's ferocious counterattack is easy to understand" given the severity of the Hamas attack, writes that "The Biden administration wants Israel to abide by the laws of war as it responds to Hamas' barbaric attack, but Jerusalem doesn't appear to be listening."

"A flood of reports challenges Israel's claims that it's exercising caution," Ward writes. "Mosques, hospitals and schools have been hit with airstrikes, as have healthcare facilities and ambulances."

"Gazans, many of whom don't support Hamas or its tactics, have nowhere to flee as the strip is under siege," ads Ward. "Shrapnel has flown into seven hospitals and 10 U.N. emergency shelters. The situation has gotten so bad that the Red

Cross said hospitals, already low on electricity, water and supplies, risk turning into morgues."

Of course Israel isn't abiding by the rules of war. They're not even pretending to. Human Rights Watch has just issued a statement decrying Israel's "unlawfully indiscriminate" use of white phosphorus in Gaza and in Lebanon, and an Israeli security official told the Israeli press that the IDF's plan is to turn Gaza into "a city of tents" with "no buildings".

This is all publicly available information, yet the western press has the gall to use the phrase "Hamas targets" when describing Israel's bombing campaign in Gaza? I'm sorry, but that's demented. The only reason to do something like that would be to administer propaganda.

The claim that Israel is targeting Hamas when it destroys buildings in Gaza is further undermined by the fact that Hamas would be taking shelter underground during this bombing campaign. As journalist Sharmine Narwani explained on Twitter, "Hamas cadres live underground in Gaza, which they have learned to do after countless Israeli bombing campaigns. The ONLY people being massacred in Gaza by Israeli terror planes right now are Palestinian civilians and Israeli POWs."

In reality, both the claims that Israeli intelligence was taken by surprise by the Hamas attack and that Israel is solely targeting Hamas with its Gaza strikes are highly suspect and worthy of intense scrutiny. Israel has never been averse to killing Palestinian civilians, and there's no reason to feel confident Israeli intelligence didn't let the attack through in order to justify longstanding agendas like the elimination of Gaza as a Palestinian territory. Both claims can be false, but from where I'm sitting it looks highly unlikely that they're both true.

If you want to support Israel's bombing campaign in Gaza then go ahead, and if you want to uncritically accept the official narrative about Saturday's attack then you do you. But don't piss on my leg and tell me it's raining.

Featured image via Adobe Stock.

People Have A Serious Case Of 9/11 Brain Right Now, And It's Scary

I had to take a short break from reading about what's happening in Gaza. I saw one too many images of dead kids on Twitter and just had to lie down for a while.

It was like running out of health in a video game. I was still trucking along, and then I saw this one particularly gruesome image on Twitter of a dead Palestinian child which I won't even describe here and my nervous system was like, "Nope, that's it, we're done," and I just felt all the energy go out of me and slumped over.

And that was just me sitting in the comfort and safety of my own home. I can't imagine what it's like to actually be there, under siege with all energy and supplies cut off, while it gets harder and harder to get information to the outside world as military explosives rain down relentlessly.

It's so, so bad, and it's going to get so much worse. Israel has already taken more lives than the 1,200 it lost in the Hamas attacks, with the official death toll from the Gaza bombings now having passed 1,200 as of this writing, on top of the 1,500 Hamas militants who were killed during the attack. But the killing is going to continue far beyond this point. One gets the sense that the IDF is barely even getting started.

That's why so much energy is getting poured into trying to make the Hamas attacks look as bad as possible—to make the gratuitous slaughter that's about to come look reasonable. We're seeing claims about decapitated Israeli babies being uncritically promoted as fact by the mass media and by US and Israeli officials, and then being walked back as it turns out those claims are unverified and dubiously sourced. We're seeing claims about mass rapes being uncritically pushed by the mass media, only to see them retracted as unverified after the narrative has taken hold.

The only reason the political/media class of the imperial core are falling all over themselves to promote these narratives without waiting for the evidence is to make Israel's ongoing murder of civilians in Gaza look appropriate. It's completely undisputed that Hamas killed a huge number of people on Saturday, and it's completely undisputed that a huge number of those killed were noncombatants. This alone could be used to justify retaliatory military operations by Israel, but because those retaliations are going to dwarf the initial offense, Israel and its allies need to frame that initial offense in the most shocking and rage-inducing light possible.

It was reported that the US and Israel were in discussions with Egypt to provide safe corridors for an evacuation of Gaza, which Moon of Alabama noted would have been ethnic cleansing if carried out. But it's now being reported that Egypt has rejected those proposals, citing the need to protect "the right of Palestinians to hold on to their cause and their land".

So they're trapped there. Two million people, half of whom are children, packed into a tiny strip of land which an Israeli security official says is going to be reduced to "a city of tents" with "no buildings". And they have to somehow not get killed amid this onslaught while somehow managing to get enough to eat and drink in a besieged city with no power.

We could be on the precipice of one of the darker entries in the annals of history.

Something very eerie happened the other day. I posted the following on Twitter:

"If I was an Israel supporter I'd be thinking very carefully about the things I'm posting online in the build-up to what could wind up being regarded as one of history's worst genocidal massacres. The internet doesn't forget. What you're tweeting today could haunt you for life."

The post received hundreds of comments, many of them hostile and argumentative. But what really disturbed me is that going through them I couldn't find a single one that disputed my claim that Israel may be on the verge of committing one of the worst genocidal massacres in world history. They were angered by my opposition to Israel, angered by my criticism of their social media activity, but apparently they had no objection to the whole massive genocidal massacre bit. That part they take as a given, and accept.

Which may come as no surprise to you if you've been paying attention to the way Israel apologists are talking about this situation. The Grayzone's Jeremy Loffredo recently posted a compilation of numerous pro-Israel demonstrators in New York City spouting genocidal vitriol calling for the extermination of all Palestinians and turning Gaza into a parking lot. It's ugly to watch, but it's also just Israel apologists saying the same things in person that they've been saying online all week.

Stokely Carmichael said "If a white man wants to lynch me, that's his problem. If he's got the power to lynch me, that's my problem." These genocidal ideations wouldn't be as much of a problem if Palestinians weren't completely beholden to the whims of a deadly military force that is backed to the hilt by

the most powerful empire that has ever existed. They can kill as many Palestinians as they've got a mind to, and there's a lot of consent for this throughout the member states of the US-centralized empire.

When announcing the total siege of Gaza, Israeli Defense Minister Yoav Gallant said that "We are fighting human animals and we are acting accordingly." This is the dehumanizing language of extermination. This is not the sort of person you want pointing modern weapons of war at defenseless civilians in an open-air concentration camp.

People are going insane, in the same way they went insane after 9/11. In the immediate aftermath of the 9/11 attacks there was this shrieking

emotional intensity which saw critical thinking go out the window and saw people's minds consumed with a rabid lust for Muslim blood. People have a serious case of 9/11 brain this week, and it's more than a little scary.

It is very fitting, then, that numerous political and media figures have been working to brand the attacks this past Saturday as "Israel's 9/11". After 9/11 everyone lost their minds and started believing a bunch of lies and consenting to power-serving agendas that went on to do orders of magnitude more damage than the initial traumatic event did, and we're seeing that same infernal trajectory unfolding again today with Israel.

Comparisons to 9/11 should make everyone more critical and resistant to warmongering agendas, not less. The most consequential thing about September 11 2001 was not what happened on that day but what happened in the days that followed, with the "war on terror" causing millions of deaths and displacing tens of millions of people—vastly eclipsing the 3,000 dead from the 9/11 attacks themselves.

That's what people should think about when these 9/11 comparisons emerge. Not "Oh well we need to consent to a bunch of military agendas and kill a bunch of people then," but "We need to be extremely skeptical about everything we're being told, and begin pushing for peace as aggressively as we possibly can."

•

It's Not The 'Israel–Hamas War', It's The Israel–Gaza Massacre
More Notes From The Edge Of The Narrative Matrix

Stop calling it the "Israel-Hamas war". It's the Israel-Gaza massacre. Calling it the Israel-Hamas war creates the false impression that this is a war that is directed exclusively at Hamas when it's really an ethnic purge that's directed at all Palestinians in Gaza.

The child body count alone makes it clear that this isn't a war against Hamas; I saw an anonymous account point out on Twitter that the number of children killed in this onslaught after one week already exceeds the total number of children killed after a year and a half of fighting in Ukraine, per the United Nations.

Laying complete siege to a civilian population and bombing anything that stands would be an extraordinary abomination in any war. And this is not a war, it's an enclosed shooting range with military explosives and human targets.

Americans should probably worry about the rapid legitimization of this idea that civilians who have a government that kills people are all legitimate targets.

According to the logic of collective punishment we're seeing circulated with regard to Gazans and Hamas, all American civilians deserve to die horribly because they permit themselves to be ruled by a regime which is orders of magnitude more violent and destructive than Hamas.

•

Hamas is responsible for Hamas' decisions, Israel is responsible for Israel's decisions. Hamas is responsible for the Hamas attack, Israel is responsible for provoking that attack via apartheid abuses and for bombing civilians in retaliation for it. It's not actually complicated.

•

Israel has been struggling with a rapidly worsening PR crisis ever since Palestinians started getting internet access and smartphones with video cameras and exposing Israeli apartheid abuses. So if you're wondering why they cut off Gaza's internet and electricity, that's why.

Israel was 100% aware that cutting off power and internet to Gaza would prevent Palestinians from recording and publishing footage of its coming war crimes. They struck a fatal blow to citizen journalism in Gaza, thereby blinding the whole world to what's happening there.

•

The mass media asked you to believe the Hamas attack was "unprovoked". Then they asked you to believe blatant babies-on-bayonets atrocity propaganda. Now they're asking you to believe Jewish kids were in school before dawn on a Saturday morning in Israel. Western journalism, folks.

•

The only reason so many Israel apologists scrambled to circulate unverified stories about beheaded babies and mass rapes instead of waiting for evidence was to make the real atrocities Israel is perpetrating and will continue to perpetrate in Gaza look reasonable and appropriate.

•

Λ **Axios** @axios

Bush on the Israel-Hamas war: "Negotiating with killers is not the option for the elected government of Israel. ... My view is one side is guilty. And it's not Israel."

WATCH our exclusive video: trib.al/tezZIZO

After this current crisis is over I'm probably going to think a lot about the fact that MSNBC suspended three Muslim reporters during Israel's Gaza assault because it didn't want Muslims reporting on it.

·

I used to think all genocidal massacres are bad but then some really smart Israel apologists explained to me that this genocidal massacre is completely different because this genocidal massacre's perpetrators believe they are doing the right thing for a good reason.

If there were two million Jewish people trapped by Christians in a giant open-air prison and placed under total siege, being told that half of them had 24 hours to relocate into the other half or be killed, nobody would have any confusion about what they were witnessing.

·

Everyone's got a serious case of 9/11 brain right now.

You know about 9/11 brain, kids? It's when something scary happens and everyone goes insane and starts believing a bunch of lies and consenting to power-serving agendas that do exponentially more damage than the initial trauma.

·

I keep getting people acting like it's controversial or even outlandish to say that Israel is an apartheid state. It's not. The leading mainstream western human rights groups say it's apartheid, as does the top human rights group in Israel.

·

They said we need more censorship because of Covid. They said we need more censorship because of Russia. They said we need more censorship because of January 6. Now they say we need more censorship because of the Hamas attack.

Maybe they just want more censorship?

·

Before engaging an Israel apologist in a debate about the ongoing Gaza purge, it's probably a good idea to ask them to clarify whether there's any amount of death and destruction Israel could inflict there that would cause them to stop supporting what Israel is doing. Is there a death count that they'd consider too much? How many dead Palestinian civilians are they willing to tolerate in this current operation? Tell them to give you a number.

If they can't give you a number and place a limit on how much human butchery they're willing to accept from Israel, that tells you they're not actually defending Israel for reasons that have anything to do with humanitarian concerns or valuing human life. They're saying they'll defend Israel no matter what it does and no matter how many atrocities it commits, because their support for Israel is entirely based on ideology and/or religion. In which case there's no reason to

continue the debate, because you can't debate someone out of their Christian fundamentalism or Zionism or Islamophobia or whatever it is that's driving their support. They're not arguing with you out of any interest in morality or justice or truth or facts, they're arguing with you solely to advance an agenda.

·

The greatest trick white anti-semites ever pulled was getting Jews to leave western society in droves and move to a far away country to spend their lives beating up Muslims.

·

There's no "collateral damage" in Gaza. Collateral damage is when you unintentionally kill civilians. You can't drop military explosives on places you know are densely packed with children and then call their deaths unintentional. It's like calling the death and destruction caused by Hiroshima and Nagasaki unintentional.

·

The US and its allies need to invade Syria immediately to stop Assad's brutal bombing of civilians, siege warfare and criminally indiscriminate use of white phosphorus. Save the children of Syria!

Oh wait it's just Israel killing Palestinians? Shit, never mind.

·

Step 1: Abuse and kill Muslims

Step 2: Wait for Muslims to respond to those abuses with violence

Step 3: Cite that violence as justification for more killing and abuse to fight "radical Islamic terrorism".

Works for the US empire's bogus "war on terror", and it works for Israel.

·

Pretty wild how the world is full of grown adults who truly believe the Hamas attack came completely out of nowhere and happened solely because some Palestinians are evil and love killing Jews.

The only reason people think Muslims are violent is because they are often born on top of oil. That's the only reason for the US empire's butchery in the middle east and its support for the ongoing military operation known as Israel, which is all Muslims there are ever reacting to. It's not okay for grown adults to believe extremist groups spring up in a vacuum in the Islamic world, completely out of nowhere, and would exist whether or not they'd watched their loved ones killed and displaced by western interventionism over resource control.

·

Israel apologist translation guide:

"You're an anti-semite" = "I cannot defend Israel's actions using facts and logic."

"You hate Jews" = "I cannot defend Israel's actions using facts and logic."

"You want Jews to die" = "I cannot defend Israel's actions using facts and logic."

"You love Hamas" = "I cannot defend Israel's actions using facts and logic."

"You side with the terrorists" = "I cannot defend Israel's actions using facts and logic."

·

Not that it really matters but for the record I personally have a great love for Jews and Jewish culture. Always have, since I was a kid. Most of my anti-war heroes are Jewish, and Jewish artists and thinkers have played a tremendous role in shaping my worldview. My criticisms are directed solely at the apartheid state which cannot exist in the way it exists without nonstop violence and war, which is falsely framed by the western empire as the monolithic source and stronghold of all things Jewish.

Conflating the abuses of that state with Jewishness and Judaism is profoundly anti-semitic. Jews are not anything remotely close to a monolith on the issue of Israel and Zionism. Most of what I've learned about Israel over the years I've learned from the brilliant Jewish people I follow who oppose it.

·

The response to the Gaza crisis from western leaders and media outlets and celebrities shows very clearly that we really are led by the least among us. The least wise. The least intelligent. The least compassionate. The least insightful. We are ruled by sociopaths and morons.

·

You are being offered two narratives to choose from:

Palestinians in Gaza are evil orc-like savages who just want to murder Jews and must therefore be caged and killed.

Palestinians in Gaza are thinking human beings who are reacting to intolerable abuses inflicted upon them.

Which is more believable?

We're being told that Israel needs to wage a relentless bombing campaign which is killing civilians by the thousands in order to eliminate Hamas, because Hamas must be destroyed to achieve a lasting peace. Every part of this is transparently false.

Firstly the premise that Hamas must be eliminated to achieve peace is fallacious; peace can be achieved by eliminating the abuses and righting the wrongs which gave rise to Hamas in the first place. There's no rational reason to believe Hamas would continue to exist in its current iteration or keep waging violent resistance if the theft and injustice from 1948 onward were rolled back, refugees had the right to return, apartheid abuses were ended, and people were no longer kept in a giant concentration camp where they are deprived of basic human needs.

Secondly the premise that you can bomb people into accepting an abusive status quo is self-evidently absurd. Even if Israel kills every single member of Hamas, there will be hundreds of thousands of survivors of this onslaught who see the depravity of Israel and refuse to accept it. You think all these orphaned boys and all these men who saw their loved ones ripped apart by military explosives are just going to be cool with the status quo from here on out? Of course not.

And Israel knows this, which is why its preferred solution is to kick all survivors of this onslaught out of Gaza and into refugee camps in the Sinai Peninsula. It knows that nothing it's doing will actually work and it refuses to make the reparations that will work, so its only other option is the elimination of Gazans one way or the other. Ethnic cleansing and mass displacement is not "peace" by any stretch of the imagination, but it might allow Israel to keep its abusive status quo intact.

Those are Israel's only real options for sustainable stability: either right all the wrongs which led to this, or go the opposite direction and inflict far more wrongs to answer the Palestinian question once and for all. It's pretty clear watching all this that Israel has opted for the latter.

·

The narrative managers are still struggling with the problem that when they announced that Palestinians had escaped from their concentration camp and killed a bunch of Israelis, an inconvenient number of people started asking "Wait, what were they doing in a concentration camp?"

·

I find nothing less morally or philosophically interesting than pontificating on how the traumatized prisoners of a horrible concentration camp should have conducted themselves once they broke free of its confines. As far as I'm concerned everything that happened on October 7 was the result of generations of Israeli abuse, the British decisions which made it all possible, and the American backing which has kept it going.

Israeli policies created Hamas. I don't mean this in the usual "Netanyahu boosted Hamas to sabotage peace and undermine its more moderate rivals" sense, I mean it in the "Those who make peaceful revolution impossible will make violent revolution inevitable" sense. If you stomp out every possible peaceful avenue of resistance, naturally you're going to see the rise of factions which favor violent resistance.

One of my most formative experiences in understanding this conflict happened in 2018 when I watched Israeli soldiers firing on protesters with sniper rifles and live ammo. B'Tselem explicitly denounced this as unlawful. There's nothing that could possibly make such a thing okay, and it was a very clear illustration of the way Israel has cut Palestinians off from all the normal pathways toward peaceful resolution.

I said when all this started that I believe the Hamas attack will ultimately be a net negative for Palestinians, but that I can't in good conscience "condemn Hamas" because nobody can articulate a positive direction that Palestinians should be taking. The fact that all peaceful avenues of resistance have been cut off is not the fault of the Palestinians, and it's not the fault of Hamas. It's the fault of the Israeli government.

Hamas is just what you get when you create an intolerably abusive apartheid state which keeps millions of people in a concentration camp whose inhabitants are cut off from basic human needs and make peaceful revolution impossible. Hamas isn't the disease, it's a symptom of the disease. The disease is an apartheid settler-colonialist project which cannot exist without endless violence, warfare and abuse.

·

I refuse to be shamed and demonized for supporting peace by people who support the murder of thousands of children.

Featured Image by Adobe Stock.

Printed in Great Britain
by Amazon